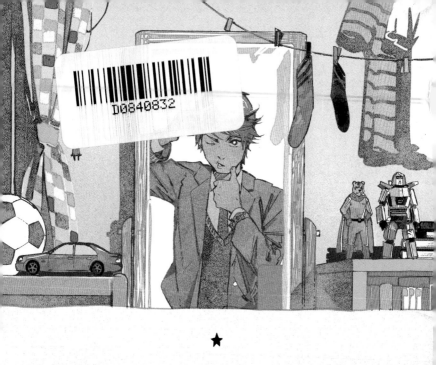

★

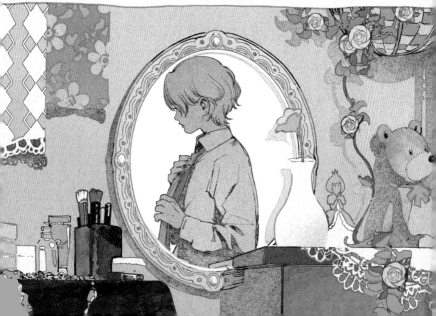

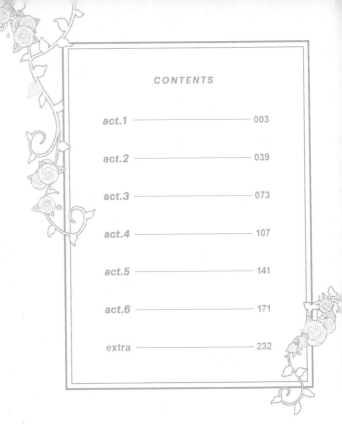

CONTENTS

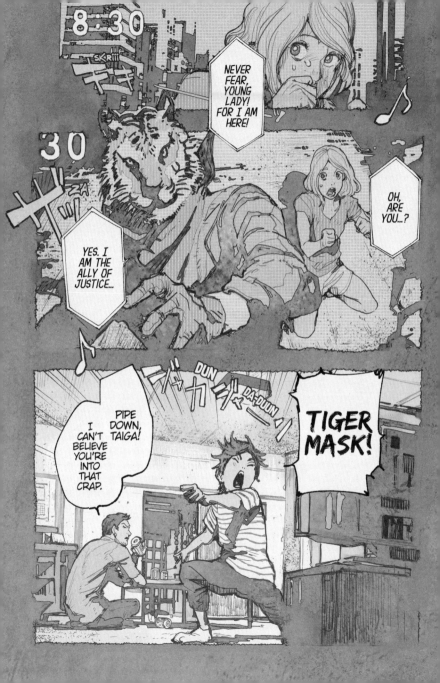

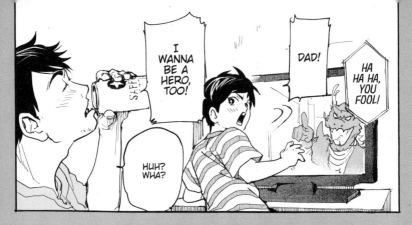

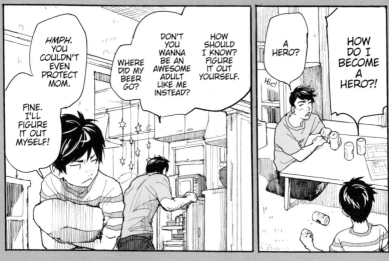

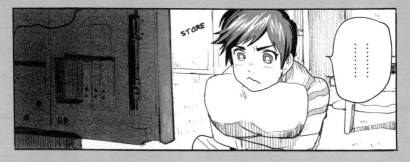

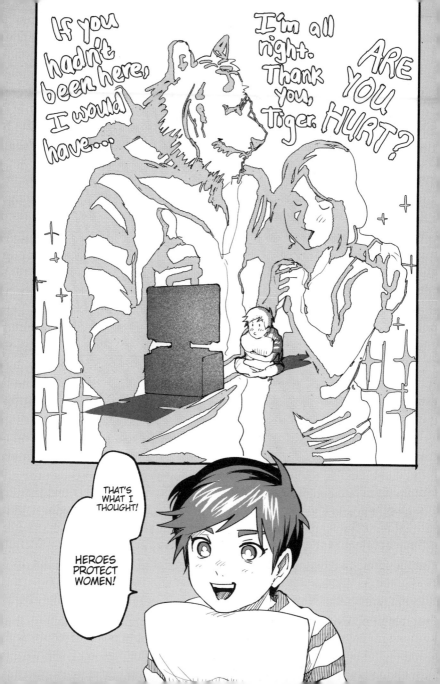

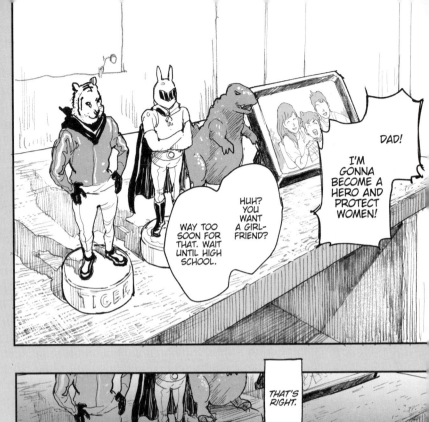

DAD! I'M GONNA BECOME A HERO AND PROTECT WOMEN!

HUH? YOU WANT A GIRL-FRIEND?

WAY TOO SOON FOR THAT. WAIT UNTIL HIGH SCHOOL.

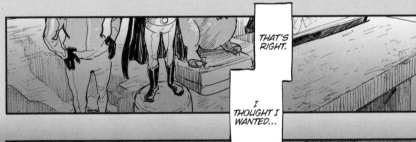

THAT'S RIGHT.

I THOUGHT I WANTED...

TO BE A HERO.

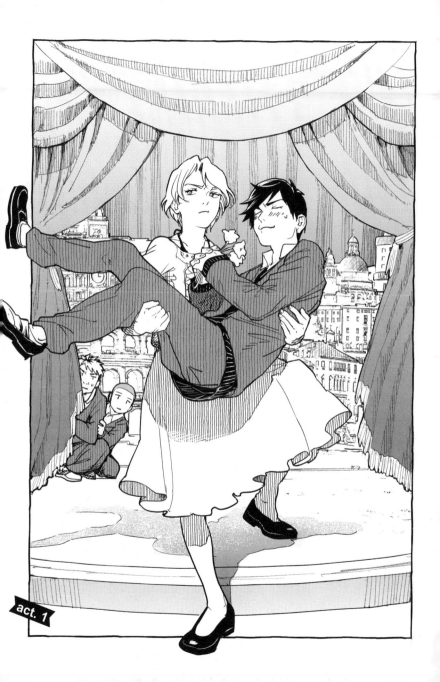

act. 1

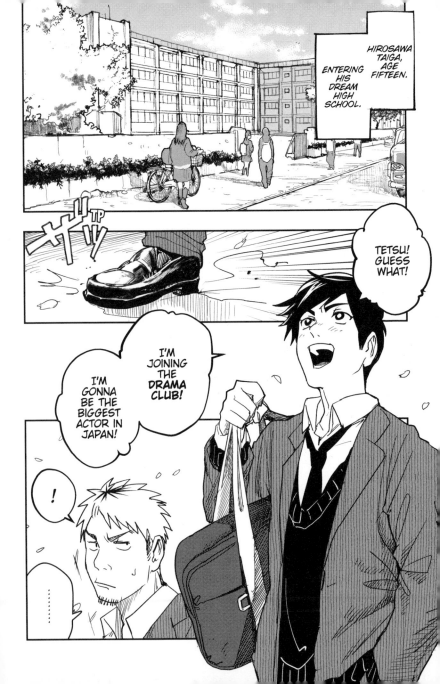

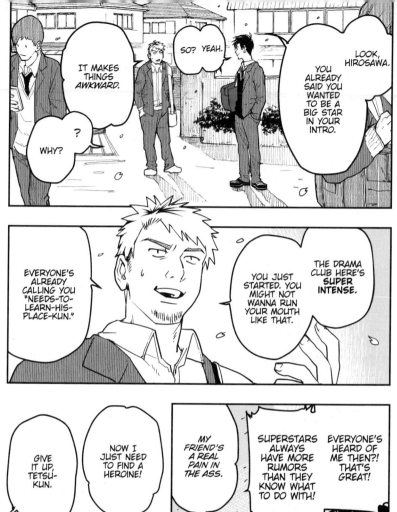

IT MAKES THINGS AWKWARD.

SO? YEAH.

LOOK, HIROSAWA. YOU ALREADY SAID YOU WANTED TO BE A BIG STAR IN YOUR INTRO.

WHY?

EVERYONE'S ALREADY CALLING YOU "NEEDS-TO-LEARN-HIS-PLACE-KUN."

YOU JUST STARTED. YOU MIGHT NOT WANNA RUN YOUR MOUTH LIKE THAT.

THE DRAMA CLUB HERE'S **SUPER** INTENSE.

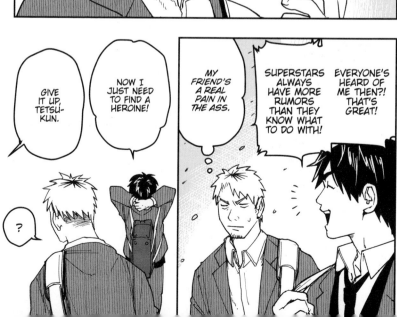

GIVE IT UP, TETSU-KUN.

NOW I JUST NEED TO FIND A HEROINE!

MY FRIEND'S A REAL PAIN IN THE ASS.

SUPERSTARS ALWAYS HAVE MORE RUMORS THAN THEY KNOW WHAT TO DO WITH!

EVERYONE'S HEARD OF ME THEN?! THAT'S GREAT!

?

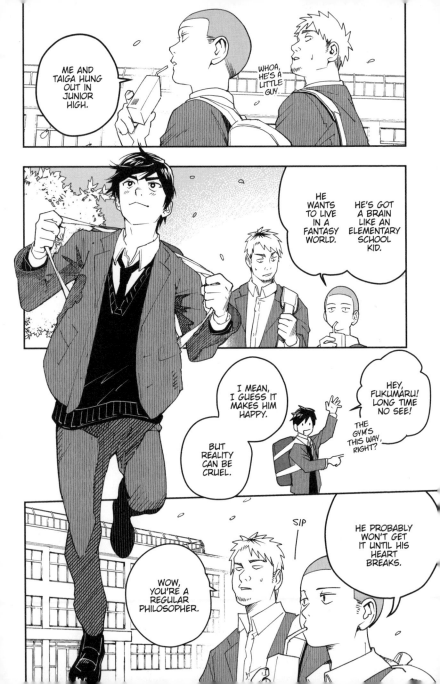

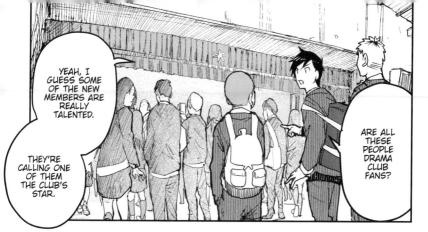

YEAH, I GUESS SOME OF THE NEW MEMBERS ARE REALLY TALENTED.

THEY'RE CALLING ONE OF THEM THE CLUB'S STAR.

ARE ALL THESE PEOPLE DRAMA CLUB FANS?

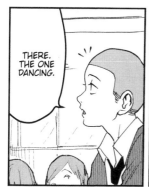

THERE. THE ONE DANCING.

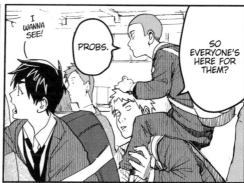

I WANNA SEE!

PROBS.

SO EVERYONE'S HERE FOR THEM?

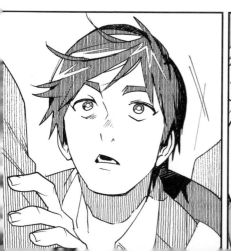

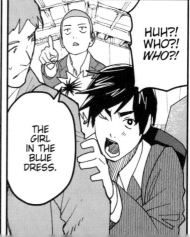

HUH?! WHO?! WHO?!

THE GIRL IN THE BLUE DRESS.

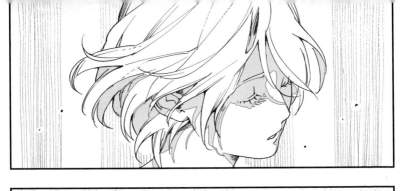

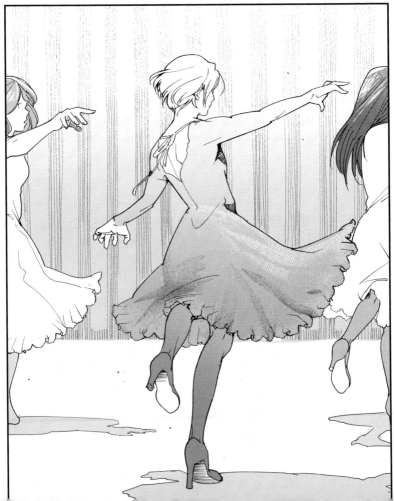

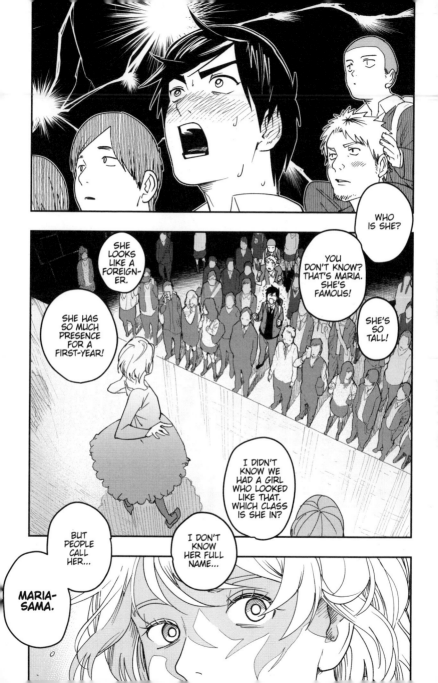

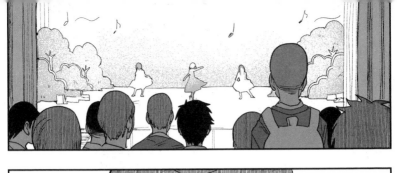

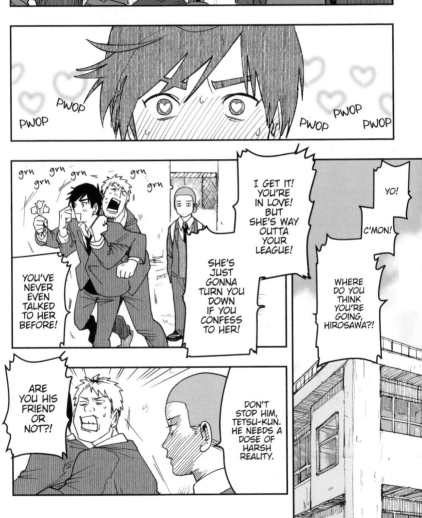

PWOP
PWOP
PWOP
PWOP
PWOP

grn grn grn
grn grn
grn
grn

I GET IT! YOU'RE IN LOVE! BUT SHE'S WAY OUTTA YOUR LEAGUE!

YO!

C'MON!

SHE'S JUST GONNA TURN YOU DOWN IF YOU CONFESS TO HER!

YOU'VE NEVER EVEN TALKED TO HER BEFORE!

WHERE DO YOU THINK YOU'RE GOING, HIROSAWA?!

ARE YOU HIS FRIEND OR NOT?!

DON'T STOP HIM, TETSU-KUN. HE NEEDS A DOSE OF HARSH REALITY.

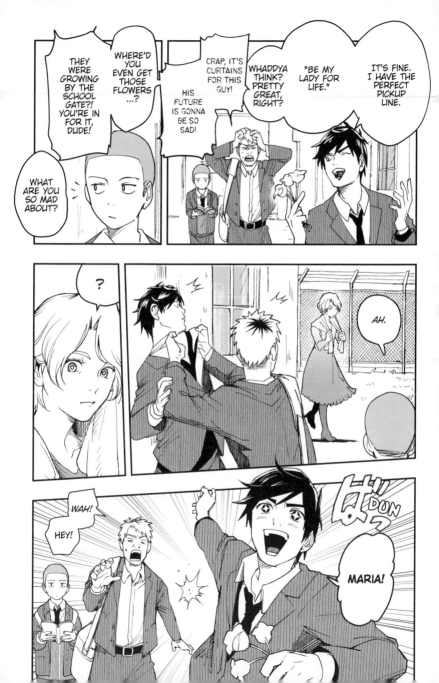

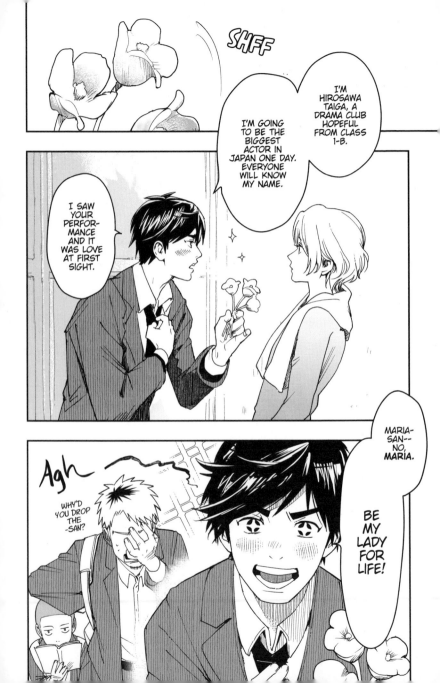

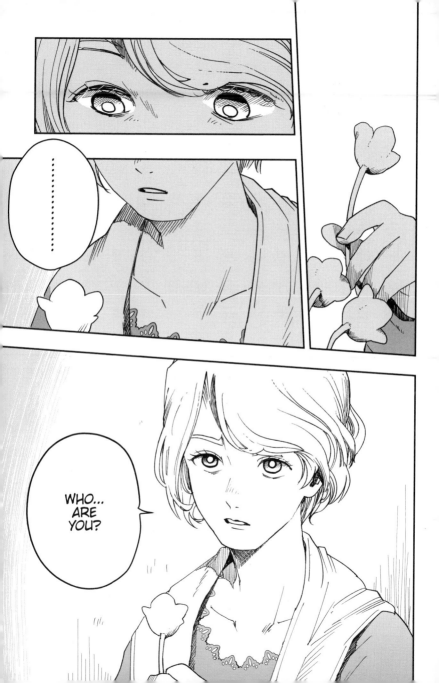

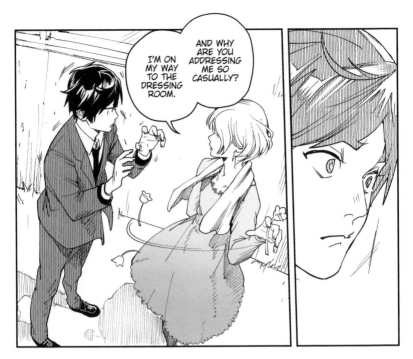

I'M ON MY WAY TO THE DRESSING ROOM.

AND WHY ARE YOU ADDRESSING ME SO CASUALLY?

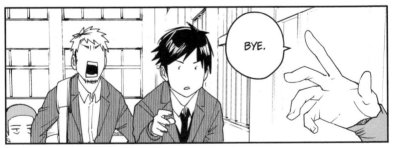

BYE.

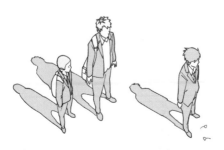

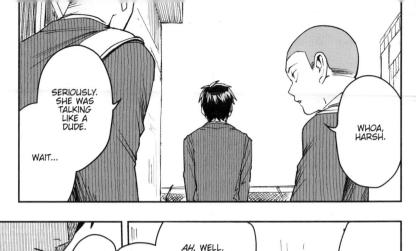

SERIOUSLY. SHE WAS TALKING LIKE A DUDE.

WAIT...

WHOA, HARSH.

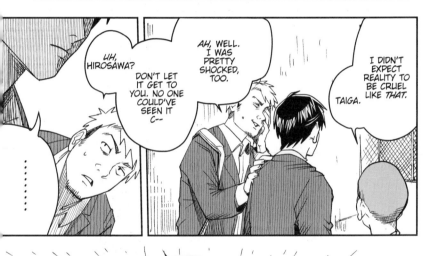

UH, HIROSAWA?

DON'T LET IT GET TO YOU. NO ONE COULD'VE SEEN IT C--

AH, WELL. I WAS PRETTY SHOCKED, TOO.

I DIDN'T EXPECT REALITY TO BE CRUEL LIKE *THAT.*

TAIGA.

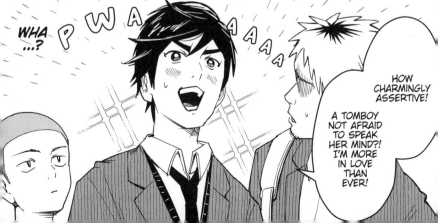

WHA...?

PWAAAAAAA

HOW CHARMINGLY ASSERTIVE!

A TOMBOY NOT AFRAID TO SPEAK HER MIND?! I'M MORE IN LOVE THAN EVER!

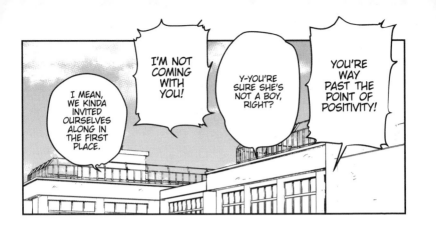

I MEAN, WE KINDA INVITED OURSELVES ALONG IN THE FIRST PLACE.

I'M NOT COMING WITH YOU!

Y-YOU'RE SURE SHE'S NOT A BOY, RIGHT?

YOU'RE WAY PAST THE POINT OF POSITIVITY!

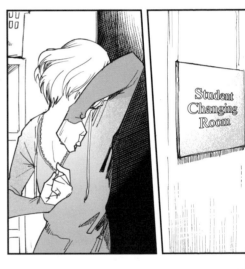

Student Changing Room

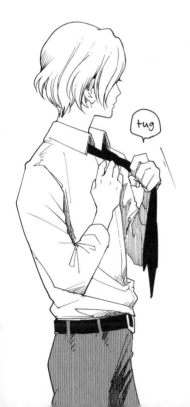

tug

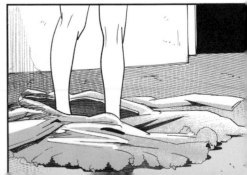

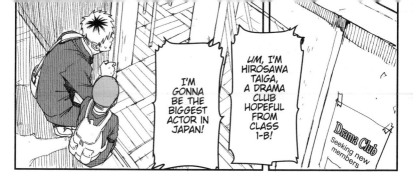

I'M GONNA BE THE BIGGEST ACTOR IN JAPAN!

UM, I'M HIROSAWA TAIGA, A DRAMA CLUB HOPEFUL FROM CLASS 1-B!

Drama Club
Seeking new members

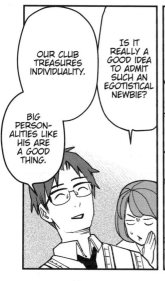

OUR CLUB TREASURES INDIVIDUALITY.

IS IT REALLY A GOOD IDEA TO ADMIT SUCH AN EGOTISTICAL NEWBIE?

BIG PERSONALITIES LIKE HIS ARE A GOOD THING.

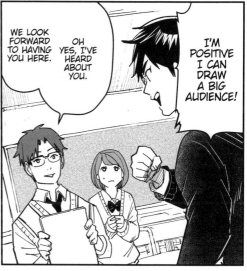

WE LOOK FORWARD TO HAVING YOU HERE.

OH YES, I'VE HEARD ABOUT YOU.

I'M POSITIVE I CAN DRAW A BIG AUDIENCE!

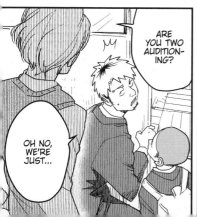

ARE YOU TWO AUDITIONING?

OH NO, WE'RE JUST...

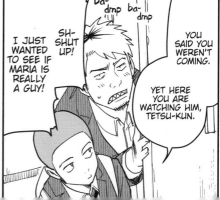

I JUST WANTED TO SEE IF MARIA IS REALLY A GUY!

SH-SHUT UP!

ba-dmp ba-dmp

YOU SAID YOU WEREN'T COMING.

YET HERE YOU ARE WATCHING HIM, TETSU-KUN.

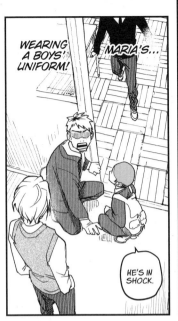

WEARING A BOYS' UNIFORM!

MARIA'S...

HE'S IN SHOCK.

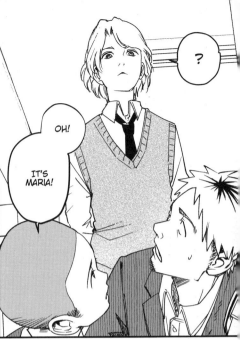

?

OH!

IT'S MARIA!

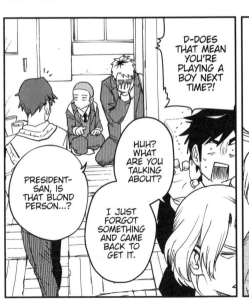

D-DOES THAT MEAN YOU'RE PLAYING A BOY NEXT TIME?!

HUH? WHAT ARE YOU TALKING ABOUT?

I JUST FORGOT SOMETHING AND CAME BACK TO GET IT.

PRESIDENT-SAN, IS THAT BLOND PERSON...?

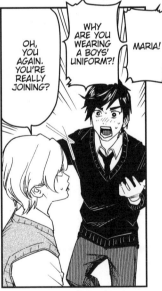

OH, YOU AGAIN. YOU'RE REALLY JOINING?

WHY ARE YOU WEARING A BOYS' UNIFORM?!

MARIA!

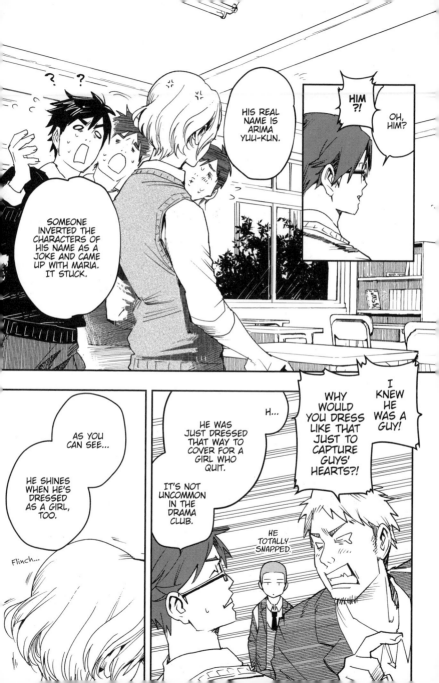

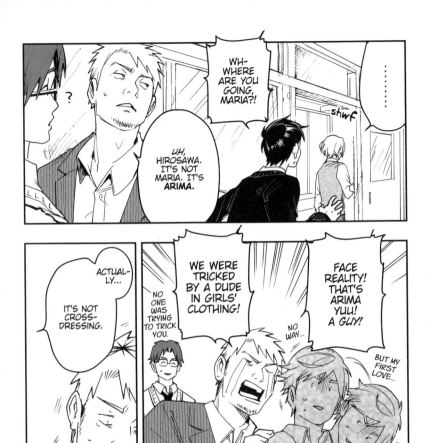

WH-WHERE ARE YOU GOING, MARIA?!

. . . . .

UH, HIROSAWA. IT'S NOT MARIA. IT'S **ARIMA**.

ACTUALLY...

IT'S NOT CROSS-DRESSING.

NO ONE WAS TRYING TO TRICK YOU.

WE WERE TRICKED BY A DUDE IN GIRLS' CLOTHING!

NO WAY...

FACE REALITY! THAT'S ARIMA YUU! A GUY!

BUT MY FIRST LOVE...

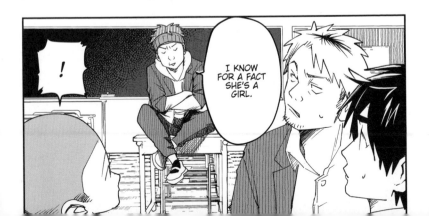

!

I KNOW FOR A FACT SHE'S A GIRL.

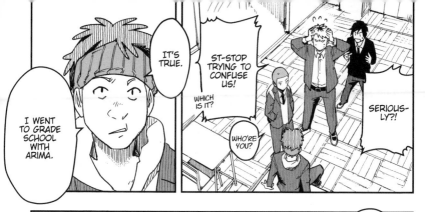

IT'S TRUE.

ST-STOP TRYING TO CONFUSE US!

WHICH IS IT?

WHO'RE YOU?

SERIOUS-LY?!

I WENT TO GRADE SCHOOL WITH ARIMA.

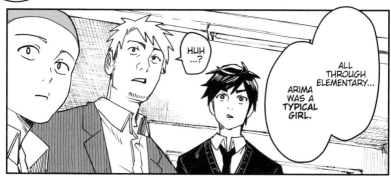

HUH...?

ARIMA WAS A TYPICAL GIRL.

ALL THROUGH ELEMENTARY...

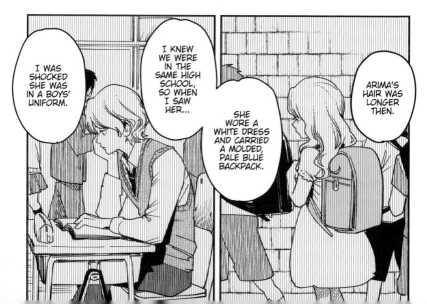

I WAS SHOCKED SHE WAS IN A BOYS' UNIFORM.

I KNEW WE WERE IN THE SAME HIGH SCHOOL, SO WHEN I SAW HER...

SHE WORE A WHITE DRESS AND CARRIED A MOLDED, PALE BLUE BACKPACK.

ARIMA'S HAIR WAS LONGER THEN.

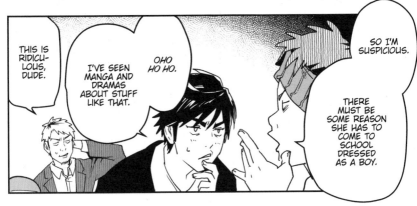

THIS IS RIDICULOUS, DUDE.

I'VE SEEN MANGA AND DRAMAS ABOUT STUFF LIKE THAT.

OHO HO HO.

SO I'M SUSPICIOUS.

THERE MUST BE SOME REASON SHE HAS TO COME TO SCHOOL DRESSED AS A BOY.

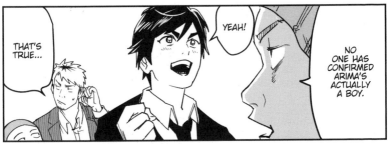

THAT'S TRUE...

YEAH!

NO ONE HAS CONFIRMED ARIMA'S ACTUALLY A BOY.

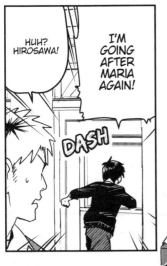

HUH? HIROSAWA!

I'M GOING AFTER MARIA AGAIN!

DASH

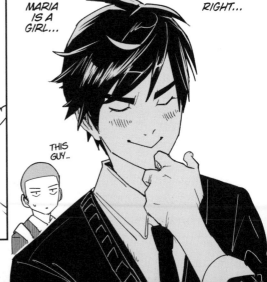

MARIA IS A GIRL...

RIGHT...

THIS GUY...

. . . .

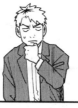

SO WHICH IS ARIMA REALLY? A BOY OR A GIRL?

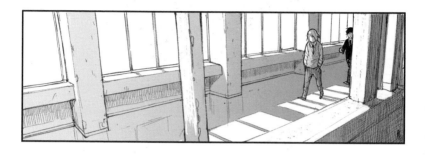

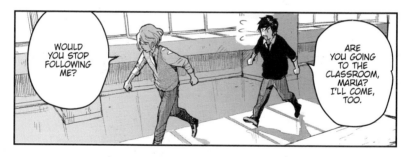
WOULD YOU STOP FOLLOWING ME?

ARE YOU GOING TO THE CLASSROOM, MARIA? I'LL COME, TOO.

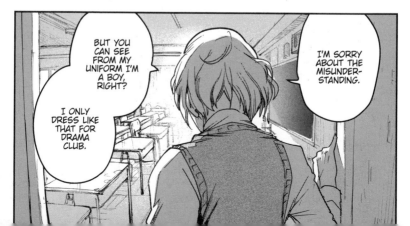
BUT YOU CAN SEE FROM MY UNIFORM I'M A BOY, RIGHT?

I ONLY DRESS LIKE THAT FOR DRAMA CLUB.

I'M SORRY ABOUT THE MISUNDER-STANDING.

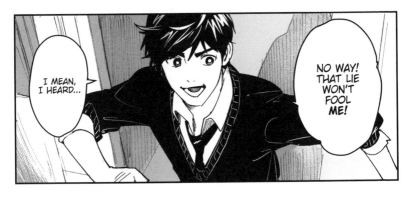

I MEAN, I HEARD...

NO WAY! THAT LIE WON'T FOOL ME!

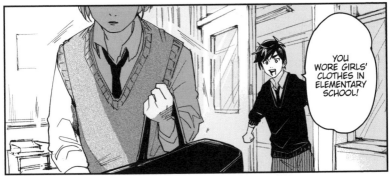

YOU WORE GIRLS' CLOTHES IN ELEMENTARY SCHOOL!

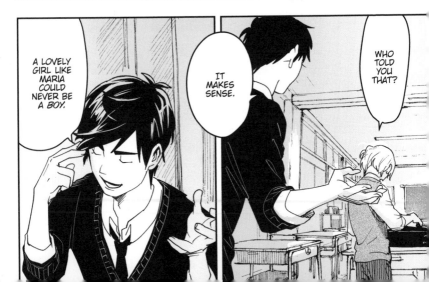

A LOVELY GIRL LIKE MARIA COULD NEVER BE A *BOY*.

IT MAKES SENSE.

WHO TOLD YOU THAT?

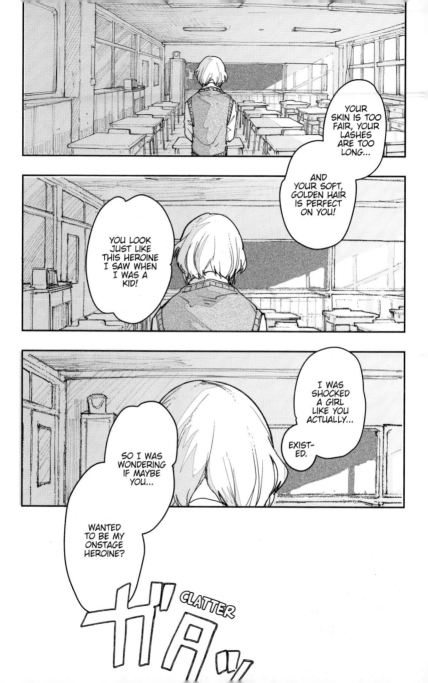

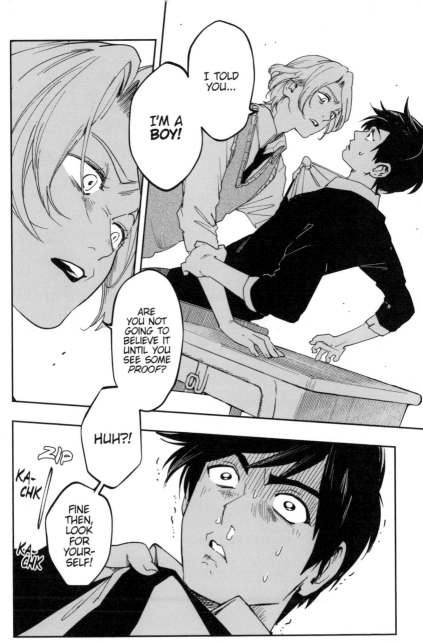

30

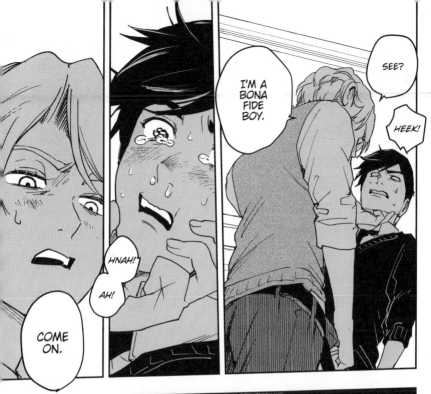
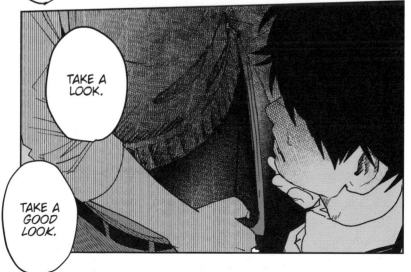

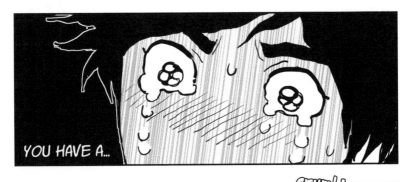

YOU HAVE A...

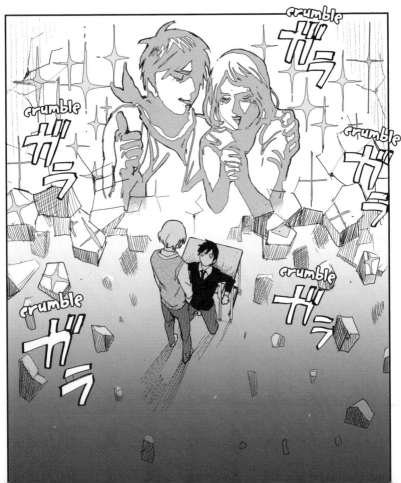

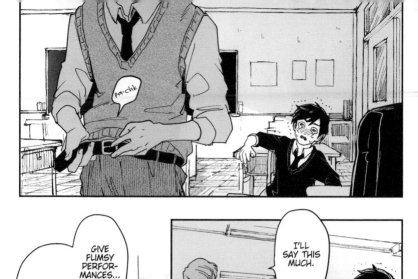

pa-chk

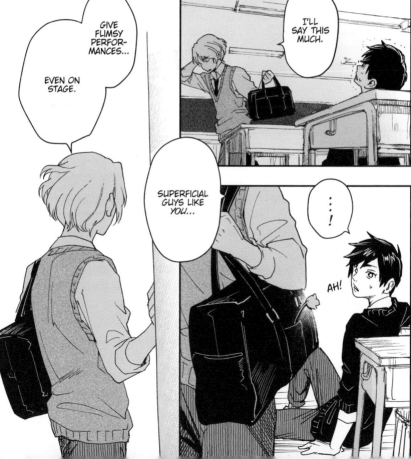

I'LL SAY THIS MUCH.

GIVE FLIMSY PERFOR- MANCES...

EVEN ON STAGE.

SUPERFICIAL GUYS LIKE YOU...

...!

AH!

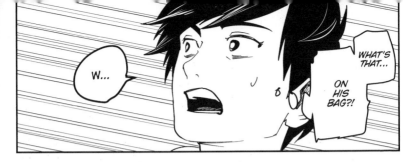

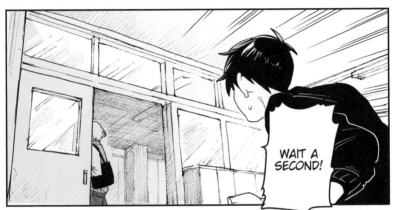

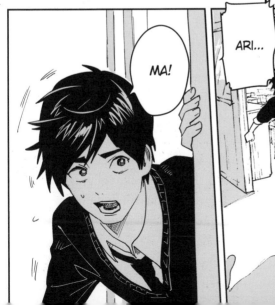

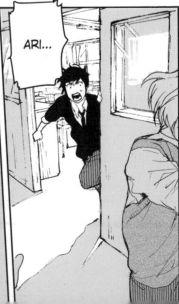

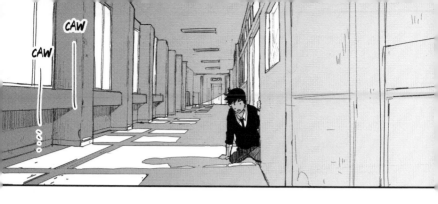

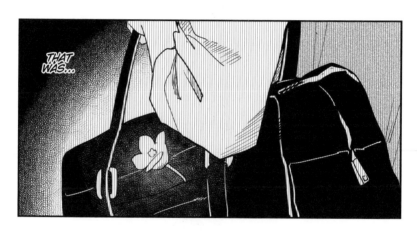

THAT WAS...

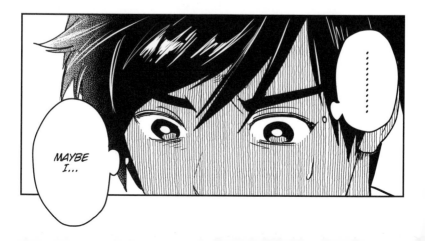

MAYBE I...

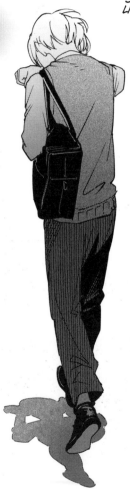

JUST DID SOMETHING LIGHT-YEARS AWAY...

FROM WHAT A HERO WOULD DO.

Boy Meets Maria

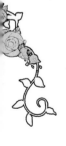

Boy Meets Maria

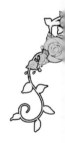

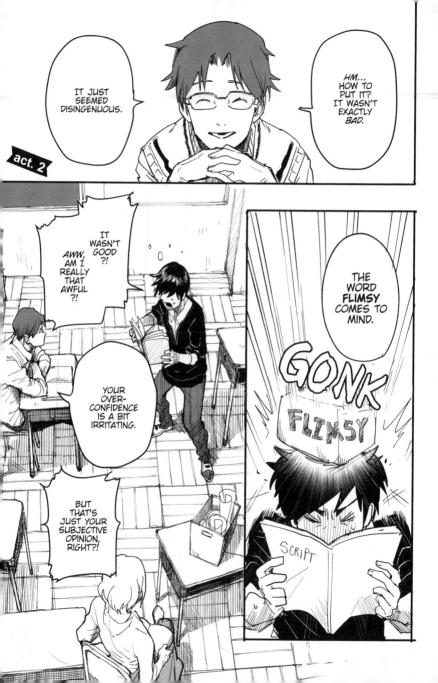

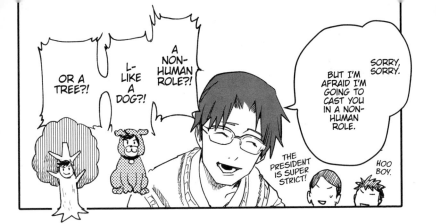

OR A TREE?!

L-LIKE A DOG?!

A NON-HUMAN ROLE?!

SORRY, SORRY.

BUT I'M AFRAID I'M GOING TO CAST YOU IN A NON-HUMAN ROLE.

THE PRESIDENT IS SUPER STRICT!

HOO BOY.

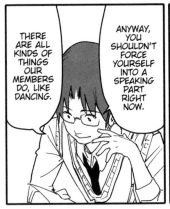

THERE ARE ALL KINDS OF THINGS OUR MEMBERS DO, LIKE DANCING.

ANYWAY, YOU SHOULDN'T FORCE YOURSELF INTO A SPEAKING PART RIGHT NOW.

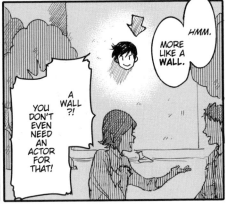

HMM.

MORE LIKE A WALL.

A WALL?!

YOU DON'T EVEN NEED AN ACTOR FOR THAT!

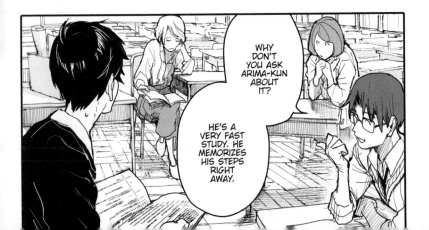

WHY DON'T YOU ASK ARIMA-KUN ABOUT IT?

HE'S A VERY FAST STUDY. HE MEMORIZES HIS STEPS RIGHT AWAY.

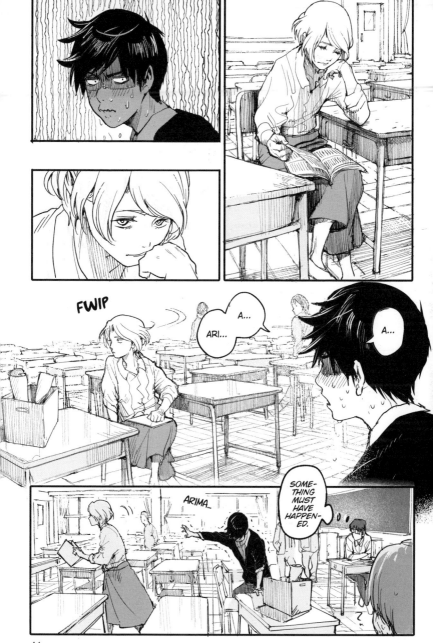

41

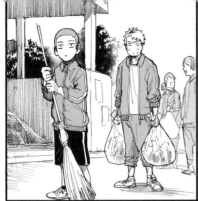

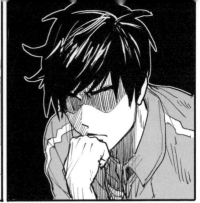

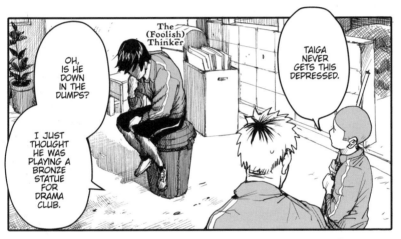

The (Foolish) Thinker

OH, IS HE DOWN IN THE DUMPS?

I JUST THOUGHT HE WAS PLAYING A BRONZE STATUE FOR DRAMA CLUB.

TAIGA NEVER GETS THIS DEPRESSED.

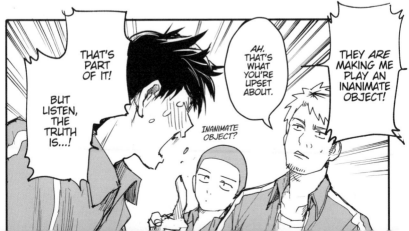

THAT'S PART OF IT!

BUT LISTEN, THE TRUTH IS...!

AH. THAT'S WHAT YOU'RE UPSET ABOUT.

INANIMATE OBJECT?

THEY *ARE* MAKING ME PLAY AN INANIMATE OBJECT!

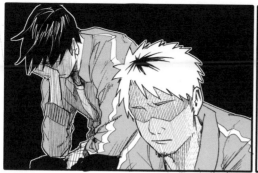

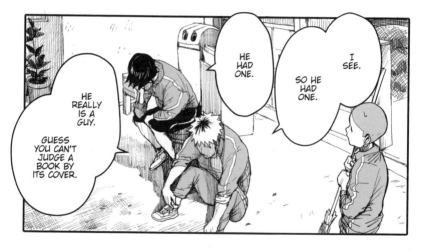

HE HAD ONE.

SO HE HAD ONE.

I SEE.

HE REALLY IS A GUY.

GUESS YOU CAN'T JUDGE A BOOK BY ITS COVER.

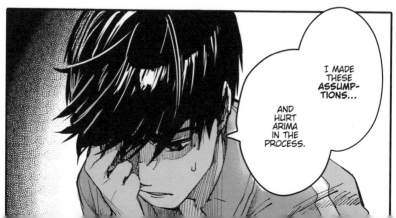

I MADE THESE **ASSUMPTIONS...**

AND HURT ARIMA IN THE PROCESS.

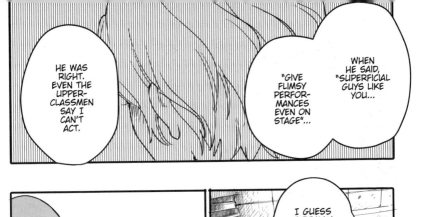

HE WAS RIGHT. EVEN THE UPPER-CLASSMEN SAY I CAN'T ACT.

"GIVE FLIMSY PERFORMANCES EVEN ON STAGE"...

WHEN HE SAID, "SUPERFICIAL GUYS LIKE YOU...

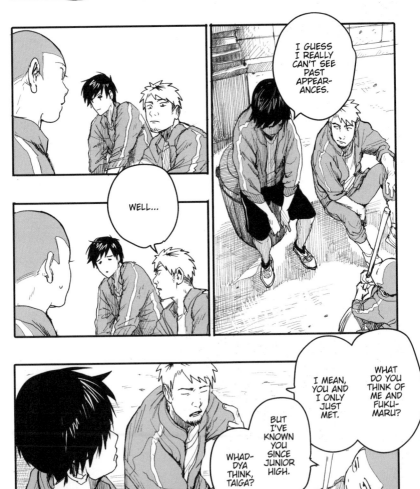

I GUESS I REALLY CAN'T SEE PAST APPEARANCES.

WELL...

WHAT DO YOU THINK OF ME AND FUKU-MARU?

I MEAN, YOU AND I ONLY JUST MET.

BUT I'VE KNOWN YOU SINCE JUNIOR HIGH.

WHAD-DYA THINK, TAIGA?

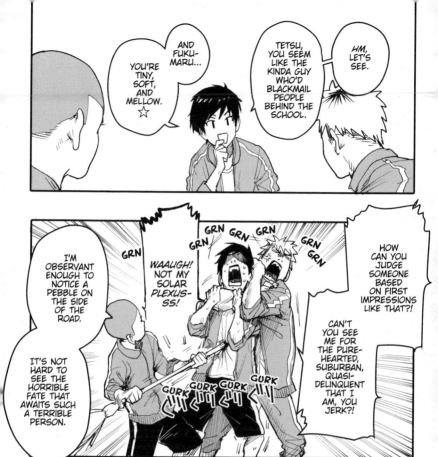

AND FUKU-MARU...

YOU'RE TINY, SOFT, AND MELLOW. ☆

TETSU, YOU SEEM LIKE THE KINDA GUY WHO'D BLACKMAIL PEOPLE BEHIND THE SCHOOL.

HM, LET'S SEE.

I'M OBSERVANT ENOUGH TO NOTICE A PEBBLE ON THE SIDE OF THE ROAD.

IT'S NOT HARD TO SEE THE HORRIBLE FATE THAT AWAITS SUCH A TERRIBLE PERSON.

WAALIGH! NOT MY SOLAR PLEXUS-SS!

GRN GRN GRN GRN GRN GRN GRN

GURK GURK GURK GURK

HOW CAN YOU JUDGE SOMEONE BASED ON FIRST IMPRESSIONS LIKE THAT?!

CAN'T YOU SEE ME FOR THE PURE-HEARTED, SUBURBAN, QUASI-DELINQUENT THAT I AM, YOU JERK?!

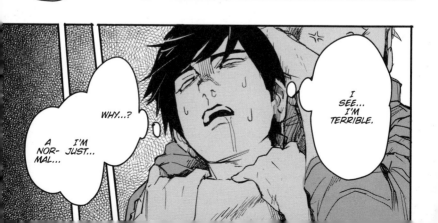

A NOR-MAL...

I'M JUST...

WHY...?

I SEE... I'M TERRIBLE.

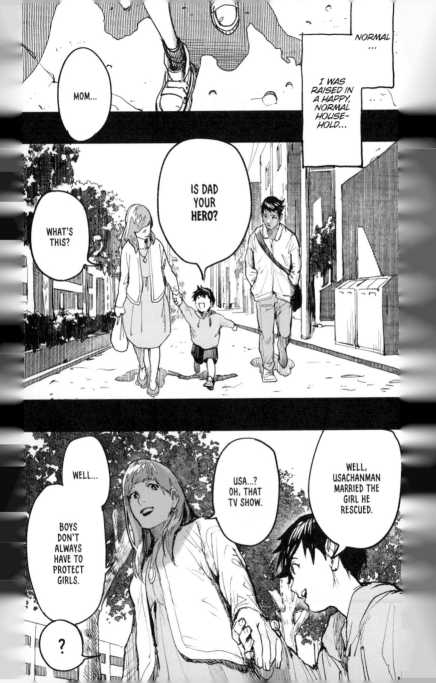

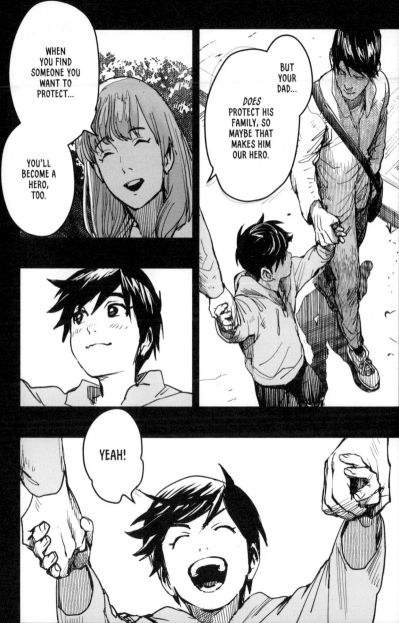

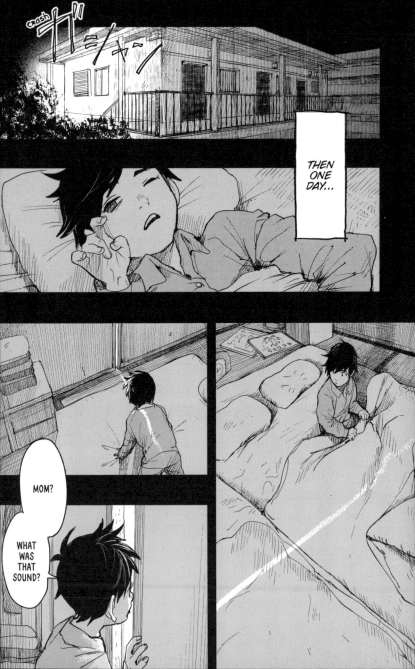

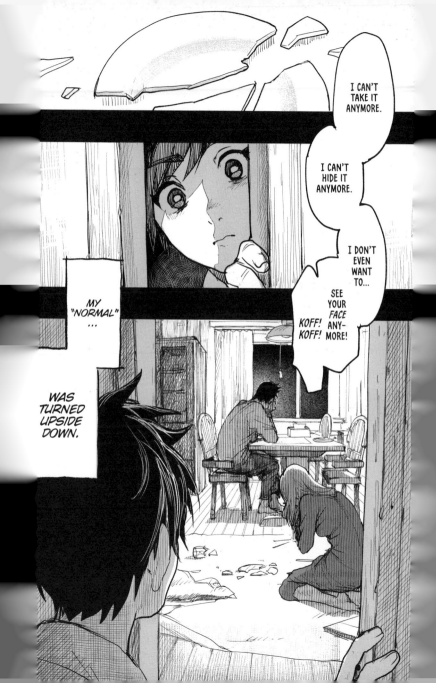

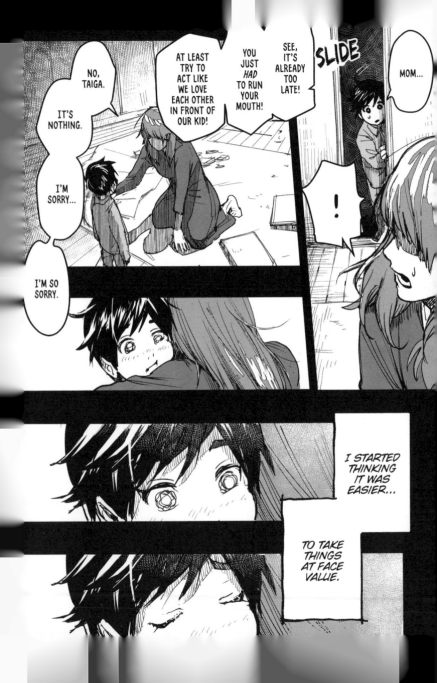

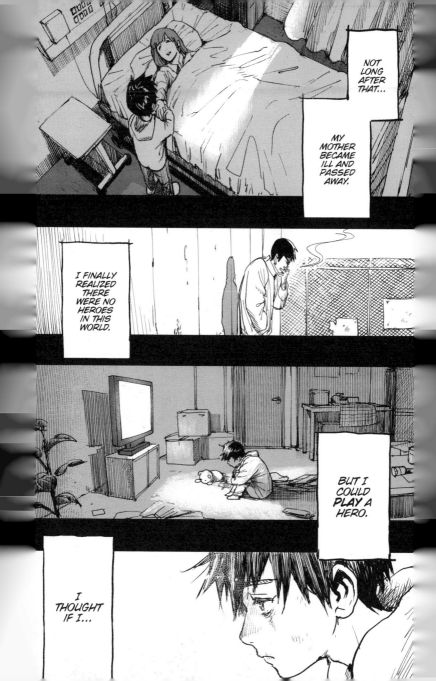

NOT LONG AFTER THAT...

MY MOTHER BECAME ILL AND PASSED AWAY.

I FINALLY REALIZED THERE WERE NO HEROES IN THIS WORLD.

BUT I COULD PLAY A HERO.

I THOUGHT IF I...

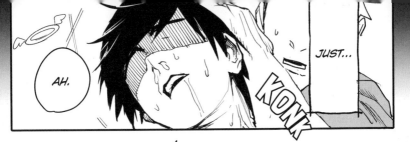

AH.

JUST...

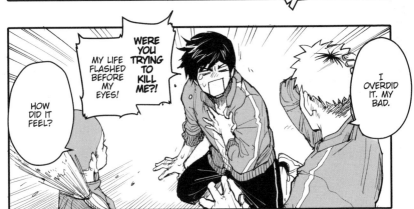

MY LIFE FLASHED BEFORE MY EYES!

WERE YOU TRYING TO KILL ME?!

HOW DID IT FEEL?

I OVERDID IT. MY BAD.

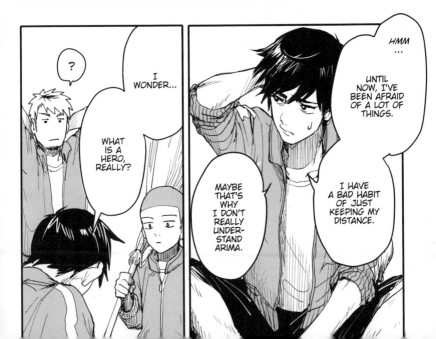

?

I WONDER...

WHAT IS A HERO, REALLY?

MAYBE THAT'S WHY I DON'T REALLY UNDERSTAND ARIMA.

HMM...

UNTIL NOW, I'VE BEEN AFRAID OF A LOT OF THINGS.

I HAVE A BAD HABIT OF JUST KEEPING MY DISTANCE.

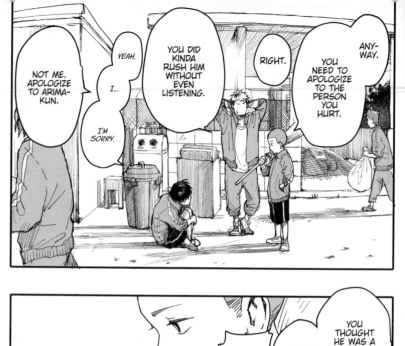

NOT ME. APOLOGIZE TO ARIMA-KUN.

YEAH.

I...

I'M SORRY.

YOU DID KINDA RUSH HIM WITHOUT EVEN LISTENING.

RIGHT.

YOU NEED TO APOLOGIZE TO THE PERSON YOU HURT.

ANYWAY.

BUT I--!

FROM NOW ON, JUST BE MORE--

YOU THOUGHT HE WAS A GIRL AND FELL FOR HIM.

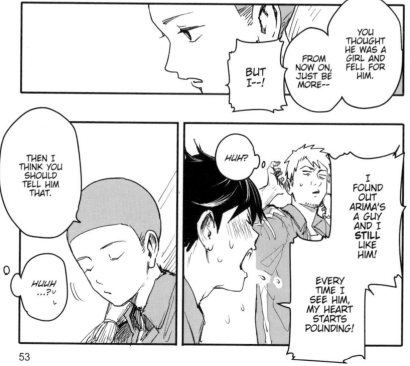

THEN I THINK YOU SHOULD TELL HIM THAT.

HUUH...?

HUH?

I FOUND OUT ARIMA'S A GUY AND I **STILL** LIKE HIM!

EVERY TIME I SEE HIM, MY HEART STARTS POUNDING!

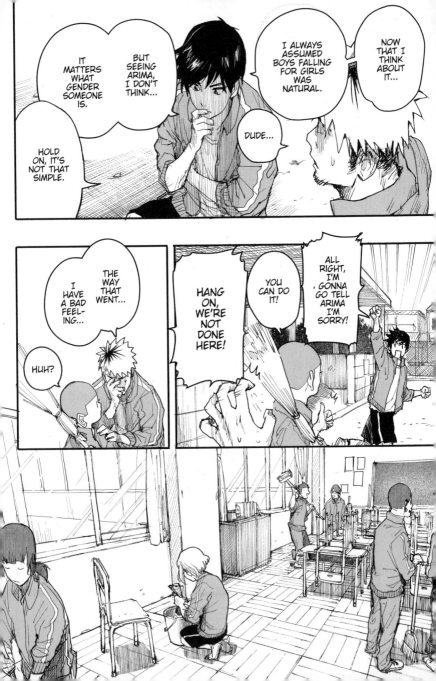

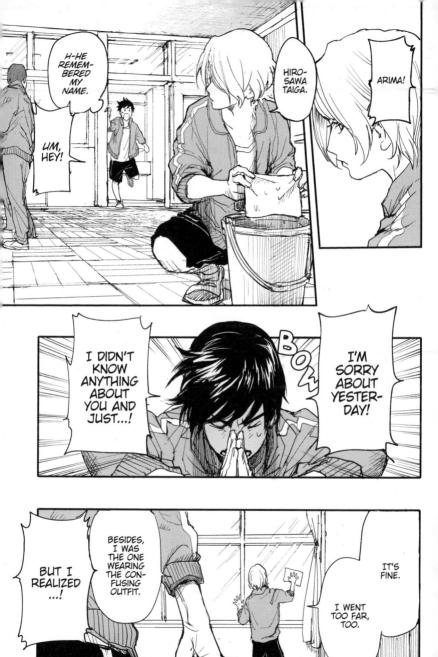

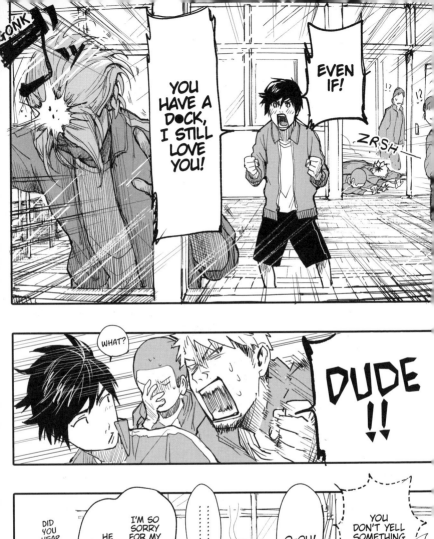

YOU HAVE A D●CK, I STILL LOVE YOU!

EVEN IF!

KONK

ZRSH

WHAT?

DUDE!!

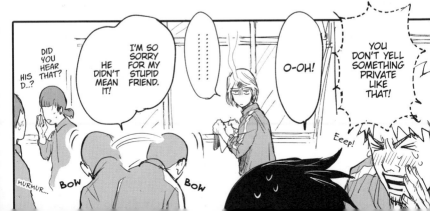

DID YOU HEAR THAT?

HIS D...?

HE DIDN'T MEAN IT!

I'M SO SORRY FOR MY STUPID FRIEND.

:::::

O-OH!

YOU DON'T YELL SOMETHING PRIVATE LIKE THAT!

Eeep!

MURMUR...

BOW

BOW

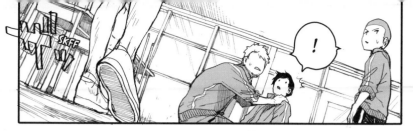

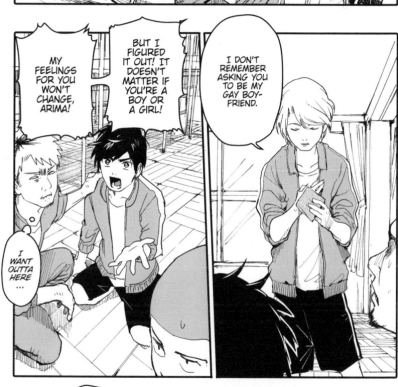

MY FEELINGS FOR YOU WON'T CHANGE, ARIMA!

BUT I FIGURED IT OUT! IT DOESN'T MATTER IF YOU'RE A BOY OR A GIRL!

I DON'T REMEMBER ASKING YOU TO BE MY GAY BOY-FRIEND.

I WANT OUTTA HERE...

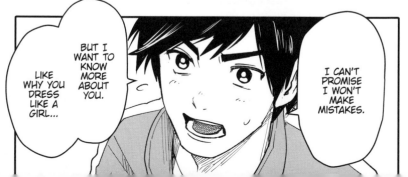

LIKE WHY YOU DRESS LIKE A GIRL...

BUT I WANT TO KNOW MORE ABOUT YOU.

I CAN'T PROMISE I WON'T MAKE MISTAKES.

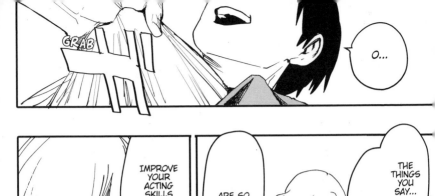

O...

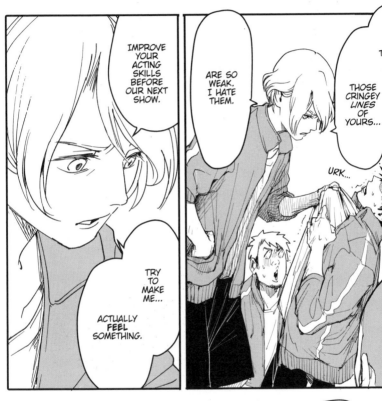

IMPROVE YOUR ACTING SKILLS BEFORE OUR NEXT SHOW.

TRY TO MAKE ME...

ACTUALLY FEEL SOMETHING.

ARE SO WEAK. I HATE THEM.

THE THINGS YOU SAY...

THOSE CRINGEY LINES OF YOURS...

URK...

?!

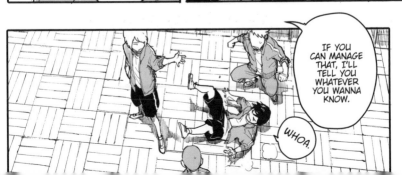

IF YOU CAN MANAGE THAT, I'LL TELL YOU WHATEVER YOU WANNA KNOW.

WHOA.

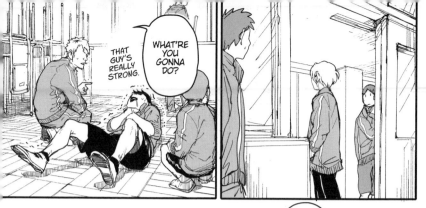

THAT GUY'S REALLY STRONG.

WHAT'RE YOU GONNA DO?

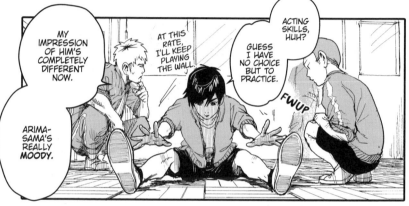

MY IMPRESSION OF HIM'S COMPLETELY DIFFERENT NOW.

ARIMA-SAMA'S REALLY MOODY.

AT THIS RATE, I'LL KEEP PLAYING THE WALL.

ACTING SKILLS, HUH?

GUESS I HAVE NO CHOICE BUT TO PRACTICE.

FWUP

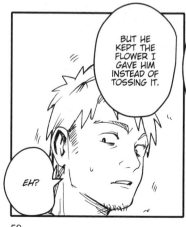

BUT HE KEPT THE FLOWER I GAVE HIM INSTEAD OF TOSSING IT.

EH?

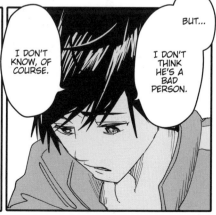

BUT...

I DON'T KNOW, OF COURSE.

I DON'T THINK HE'S A BAD PERSON.

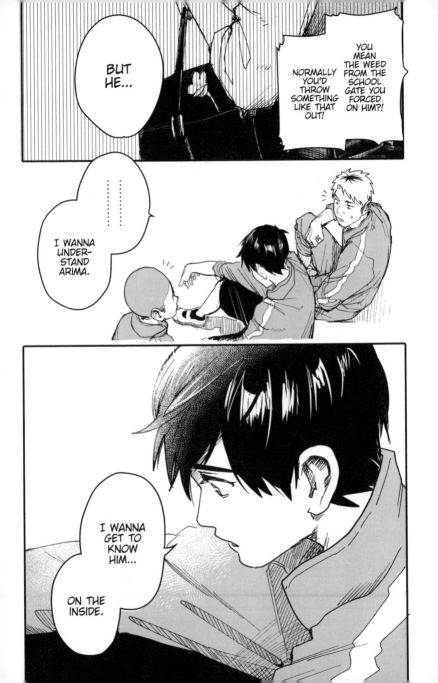

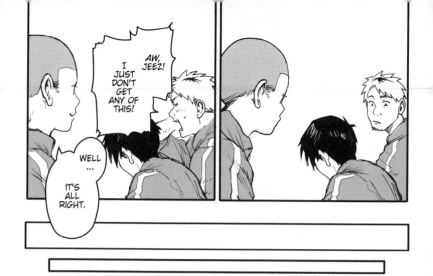

I JUST DON'T GET ANY OF THIS!

AW, JEEZ!

WELL...

IT'S ALL RIGHT.

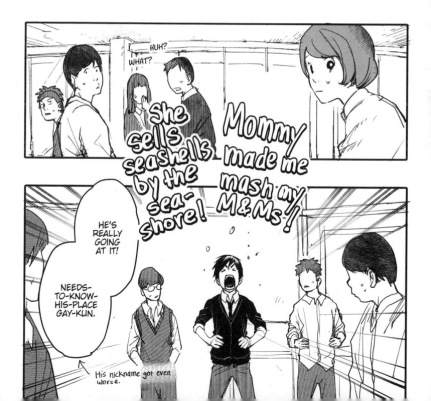

HUH?

WHAT?

She sells seashells by the seashore!

Mommy made me mash my M&Ms!

HE'S REALLY GOING AT IT!

NEEDS-TO-KNOW-HIS-PLACE GAY-KUN.

His nickname got even worse.

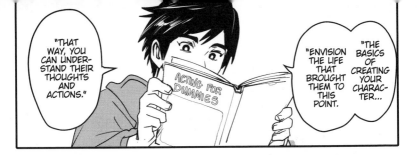

"THAT WAY, YOU CAN UNDERSTAND THEIR THOUGHTS AND ACTIONS."

"ENVISION THE LIFE THAT BROUGHT THEM TO THIS POINT.

"THE BASICS OF CREATING YOUR CHARACTER...

ACTING FOR DUMMIES

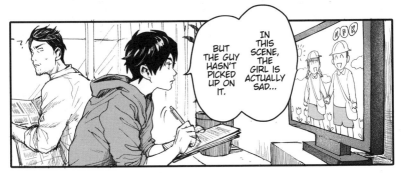

BUT THE GUY HASN'T PICKED UP ON IT.

IN THIS SCENE, THE GIRL IS ACTUALLY SAD...

N H K

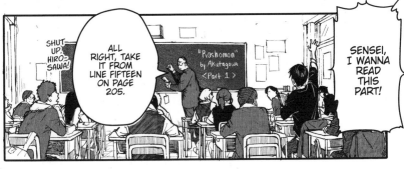

SHUT UP, HIROSAWA!

ALL RIGHT, TAKE IT FROM LINE FIFTEEN ON PAGE 205.

"Rashomon" by Akutagawa <Part 1.>

SENSEI, I WANNA READ THIS PART!

*These lines are from the short story "Rashomon" by Ryūnosuke Akutagawa.

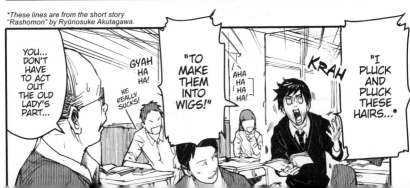

YOU... DON'T HAVE TO ACT OUT THE OLD LADY'S PART...

GYAH HA HA!

HE REALLY SUCKS!

"TO MAKE THEM INTO WIGS!"

AHA HA HA HA!

KRAH

"I PLUCK AND PLUCK THESE HAIRS...*

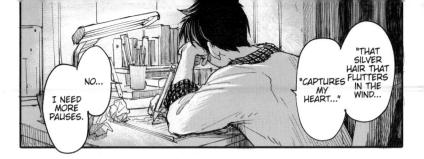

"THAT SILVER HAIR THAT FLUTTERS IN THE WIND...

"CAPTURES MY HEART..."

NO... I NEED MORE PAUSES.

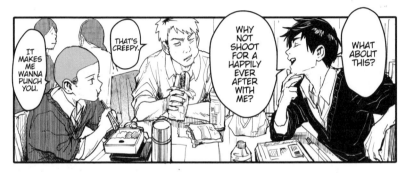

IT MAKES ME WANNA PUNCH YOU.

THAT'S CREEPY.

WHY NOT SHOOT FOR A HAPPILY EVER AFTER WITH ME?

WHAT ABOUT THIS?

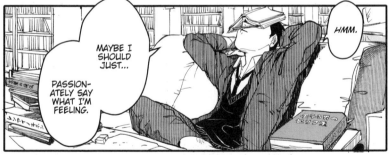

MAYBE I SHOULD JUST...

PASSION-ATELY SAY WHAT I'M FEELING.

HMM.

*He's using a line from a pivotal moment in the 1991 Japanese drama 101st Marriage Proposal.

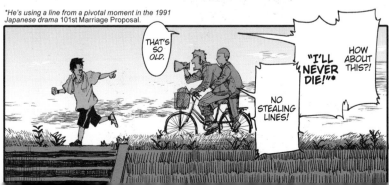

THAT'S SO OLD.

"I'LL NEVER DIE!"*

HOW ABOUT THIS?!

NO STEALING LINES!

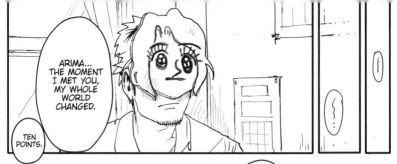

ARIMA... THE MOMENT I MET YOU, MY WHOLE WORLD CHANGED.

TEN POINTS.

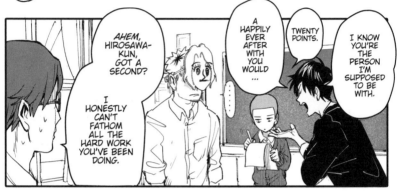

AHEM, HIROSAWA-KUN, GOT A SECOND?

I HONESTLY CAN'T FATHOM ALL THE HARD WORK YOU'VE BEEN DOING.

A HAPPILY EVER AFTER WITH YOU WOULD...

TWENTY POINTS.

I KNOW YOU'RE THE PERSON I'M SUPPOSED TO BE WITH.

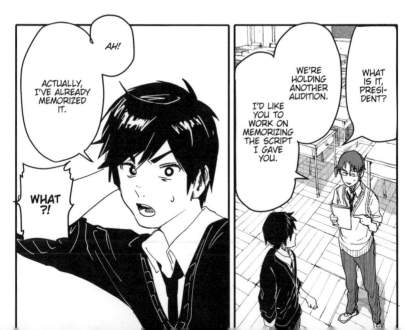

AH!

ACTUALLY, I'VE ALREADY MEMORIZED IT.

WHAT?!

WHAT IS IT, PRESIDENT?

WE'RE HOLDING ANOTHER AUDITION.

I'D LIKE YOU TO WORK ON MEMORIZING THE SCRIPT I GAVE YOU.

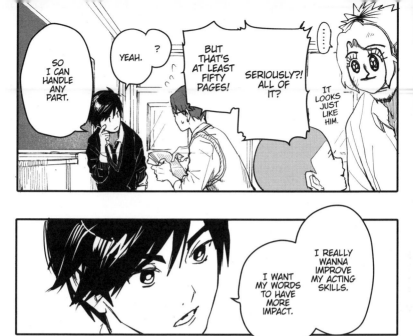

SO I CAN HANDLE ANY PART.

YEAH. ?

BUT THAT'S AT LEAST FIFTY PAGES!

SERIOUSLY?! ALL OF IT?

IT LOOKS JUST LIKE HIM.

......!

I WANT MY WORDS TO HAVE MORE IMPACT.

I REALLY WANNA IMPROVE MY ACTING SKILLS.

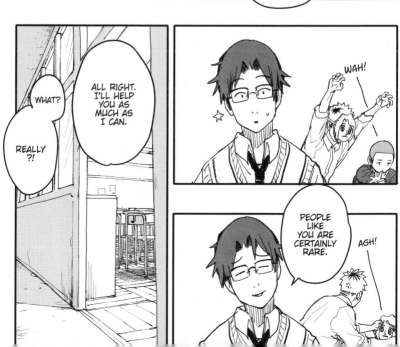

WHAT?

ALL RIGHT. I'LL HELP YOU AS MUCH AS I CAN.

REALLY?!

WAH!

PEOPLE LIKE YOU ARE CERTAINLY RARE.

AGH!

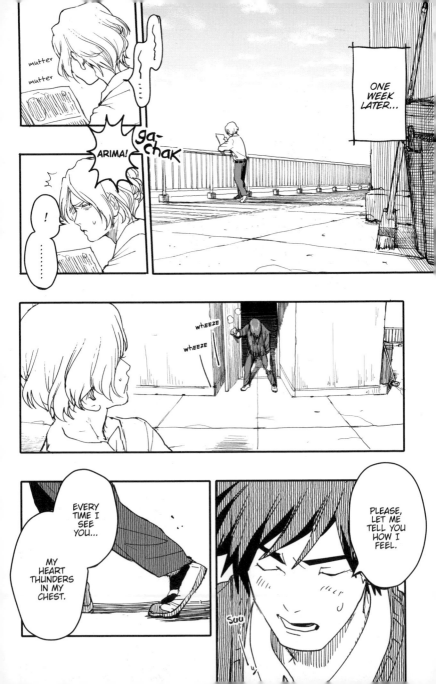

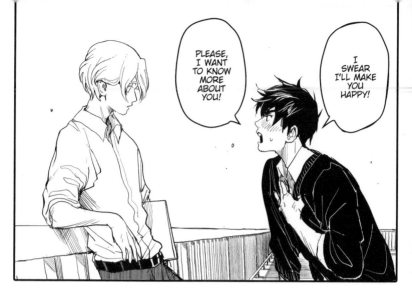

PLEASE, I WANT TO KNOW MORE ABOUT YOU!

I SWEAR I'LL MAKE YOU HAPPY!

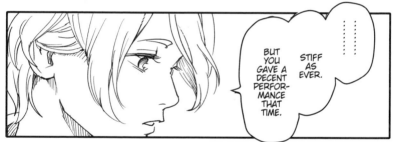

BUT YOU GAVE A DECENT PERFORMANCE THAT TIME.

STIFF AS EVER.

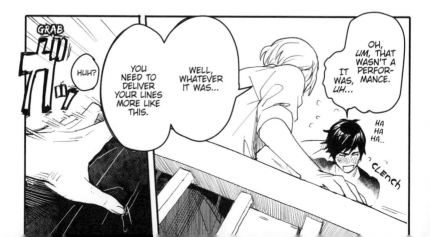

GRAB

HUH?

YOU NEED TO DELIVER YOUR LINES MORE LIKE THIS.

WELL, WHATEVER IT WAS...

OH, UM, THAT WASN'T A PERFORMANCE. IT WAS, UH...

HA HA HA...

CLENCH

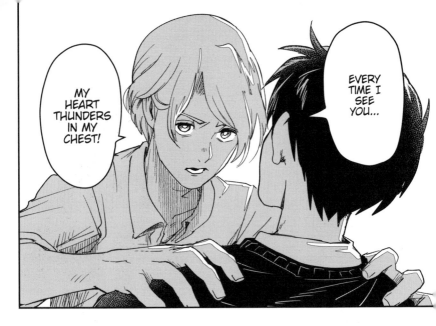

MY HEART THUNDERS IN MY CHEST!

EVERY TIME I SEE YOU...

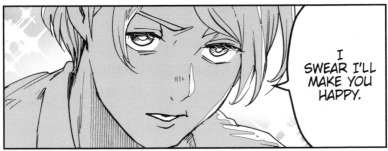

I SWEAR I'LL MAKE YOU HAPPY.

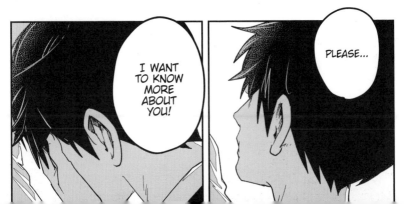

I WANT TO KNOW MORE ABOUT YOU!

PLEASE...

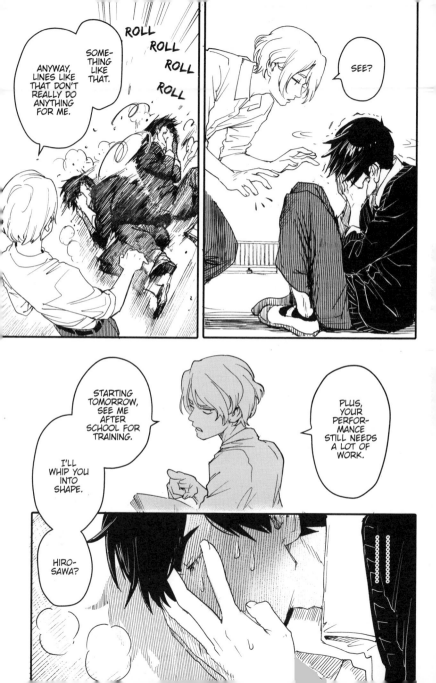

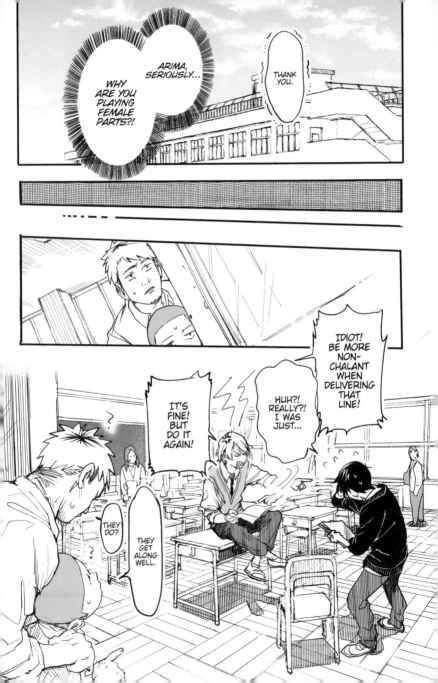

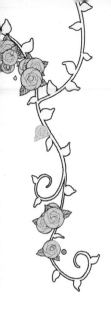

Boy Meets Maria

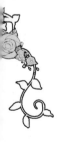

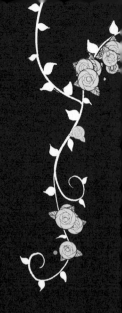

Boy Meets Maria

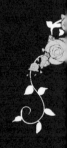

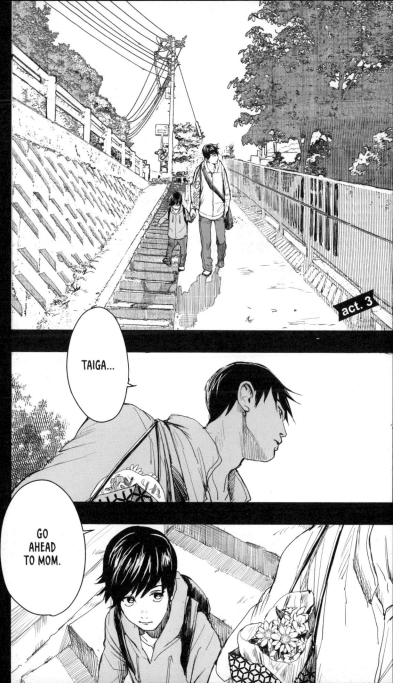

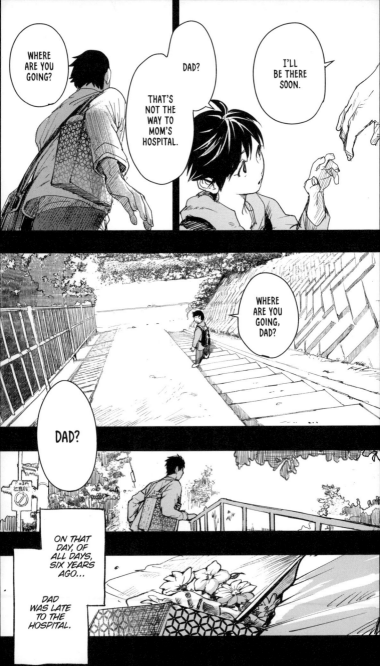

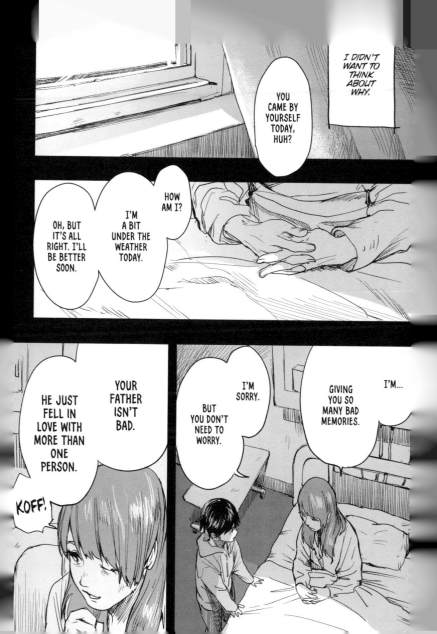

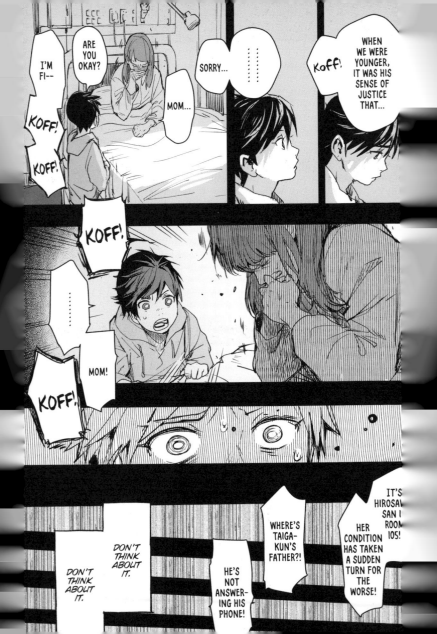

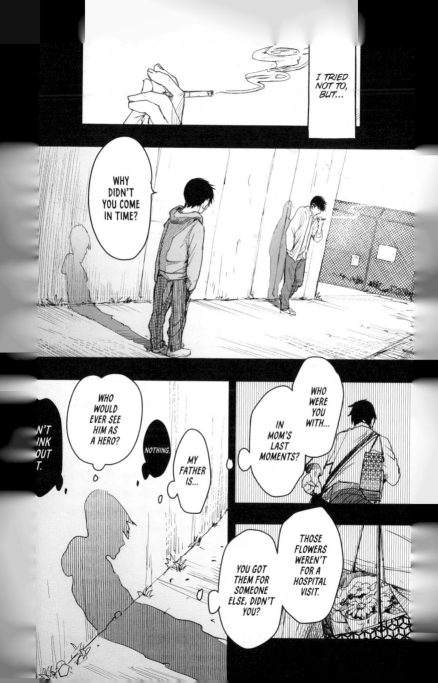

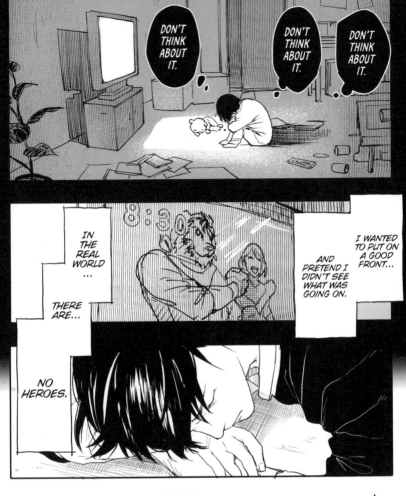

DON'T THINK ABOUT IT.

DON'T THINK ABOUT IT.

DON'T THINK ABOUT IT.

IN THE REAL WORLD...

THERE ARE...

I WANTED TO PUT ON A GOOD FRONT...

AND PRETEND I DIDN'T SEE WHAT WAS GOING ON.

NO HEROES.

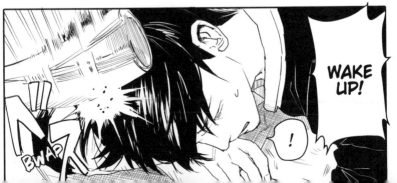

WAKE UP!

BWAP

!

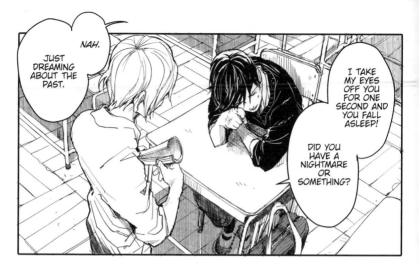

I TAKE MY EYES OFF YOU FOR ONE SECOND AND YOU FALL ASLEEP!

DID YOU HAVE A NIGHTMARE OR SOMETHING?

NAH.

JUST DREAMING ABOUT THE PAST.

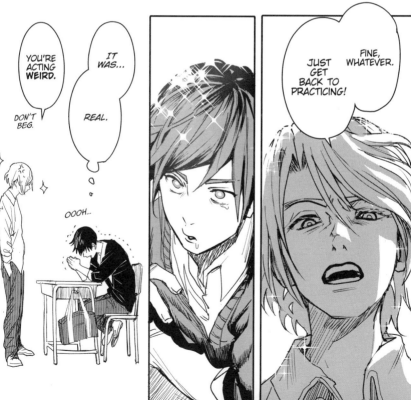

YOU'RE ACTING **WEIRD**.

DON'T BEG.

IT WAS...

REAL.

OOOH...

FINE, WHATEVER.

JUST GET BACK TO PRACTICING!

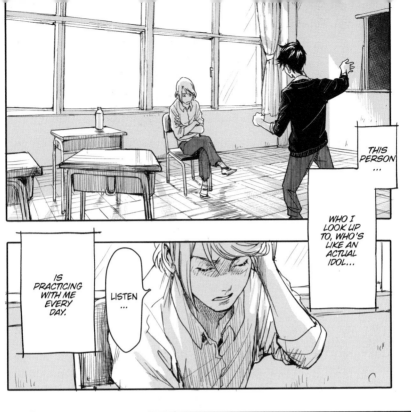

THIS PERSON...

WHO I LOOK UP TO, WHO'S LIKE AN ACTUAL IDOL...

IS PRACTICING WITH ME EVERY DAY.

LISTEN...

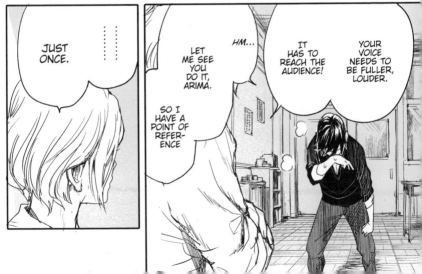

JUST ONCE.

HM...

LET ME SEE YOU DO IT, ARIMA.

SO I HAVE A POINT OF REFERENCE

IT HAS TO REACH THE AUDIENCE!

YOUR VOICE NEEDS TO BE FULLER, LOUDER.

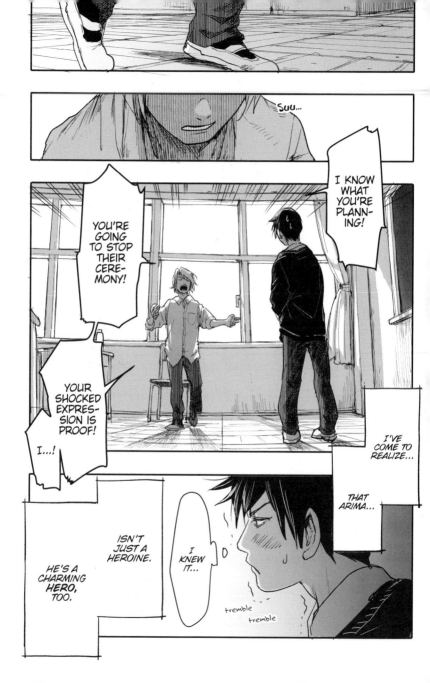

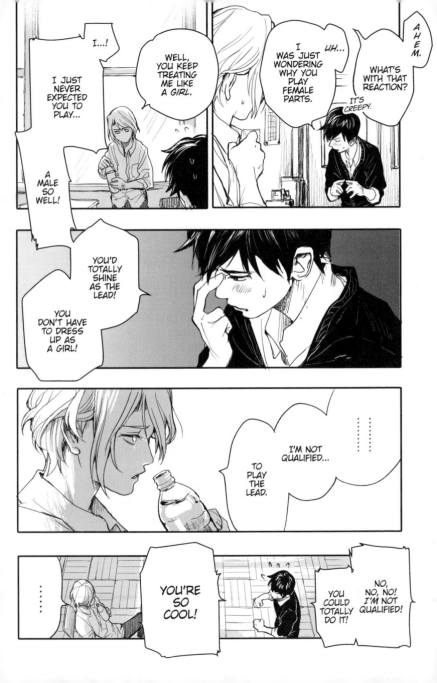

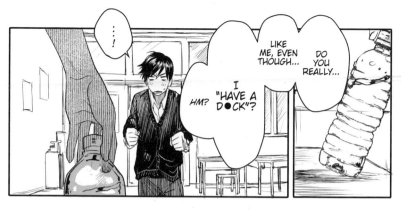

...!

LIKE ME, EVEN THOUGH... DO YOU REALLY...

HM?

I "HAVE A D●CK"?

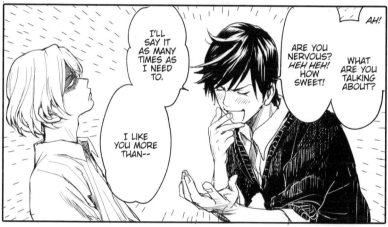

I'LL SAY IT AS MANY TIMES AS I NEED TO.

I LIKE YOU MORE THAN--

AH!

ARE YOU NERVOUS? *HEH HEH!* HOW SWEET!

WHAT ARE YOU TALKING ABOUT?

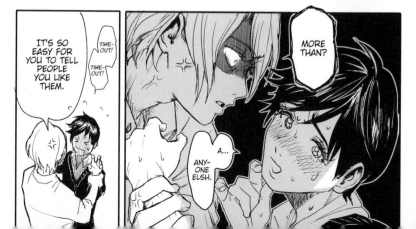

IT'S SO EASY FOR YOU TO TELL PEOPLE YOU LIKE THEM.

TIME-OUT!

TIME-OUT!

MORE THAN?

A...

ANY-ONE ELSH.

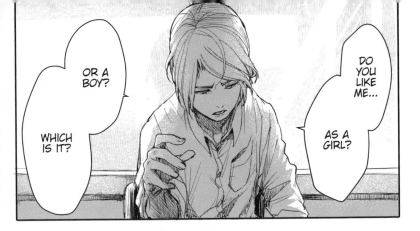

OR A BOY?

WHICH IS IT?

DO YOU LIKE ME...

AS A GIRL?

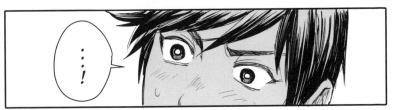

...!

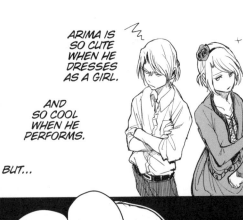

ARIMA IS SO CUTE WHEN HE DRESSES AS A GIRL.

AND SO COOL WHEN HE PERFORMS.

BUT...

THINKING ABOUT IT...

THAT'S WHERE I'M MOST CONFUSED.

....

DON'T HURT YOURSELF.

The (Foolish) Thinker

.........?

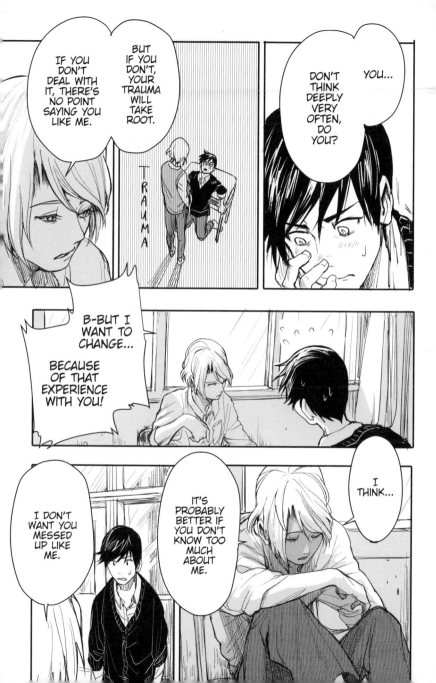

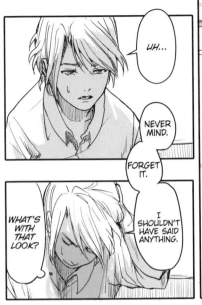

UH...

NEVER MIND.

FORGET IT.

I SHOULDN'T HAVE SAID ANYTHING.

WHAT'S WITH THAT LOOK?

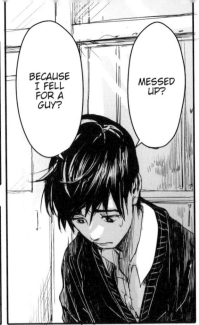

BECAUSE I FELL FOR A GUY?

MESSED UP?

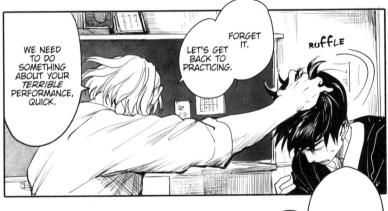

WE NEED TO DO SOMETHING ABOUT YOUR *TERRIBLE* PERFORMANCE, QUICK.

FORGET IT. LET'S GET BACK TO PRACTICING.

RUFFLE

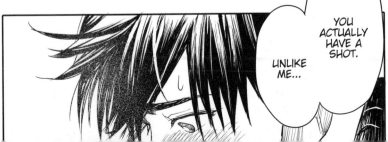

YOU ACTUALLY HAVE A SHOT.

UNLIKE ME...

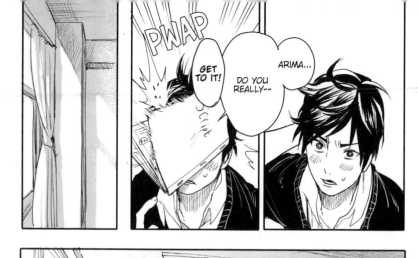

PWAP

GET TO IT!

DO YOU REALLY--

ARIMA...

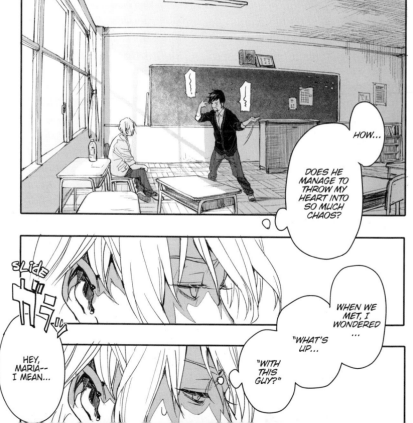

HOW...

DOES HE MANAGE TO THROW MY HEART INTO SO MUCH CHAOS?

SLiDE

WHEN WE MET, I WONDERED...

"WHAT'S UP...

"WITH THIS GUY?"

HEY, MARIA-- I MEAN...

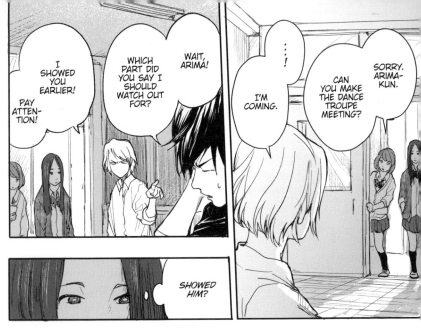

I SHOWED YOU EARLIER!

PAY ATTENTION!

WHICH PART DID YOU SAY I SHOULD WATCH OUT FOR?

WAIT, ARIMA!

...!

I'M COMING.

CAN YOU MAKE THE DANCE TROUPE MEETING?

SORRY. ARIMA-KUN.

SHOWED HIM?

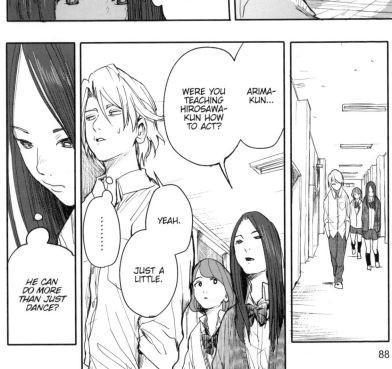

WERE YOU TEACHING HIROSAWA-KUN HOW TO ACT?

ARIMA-KUN...

....

YEAH.

JUST A LITTLE.

HE CAN DO MORE THAN JUST DANCE?

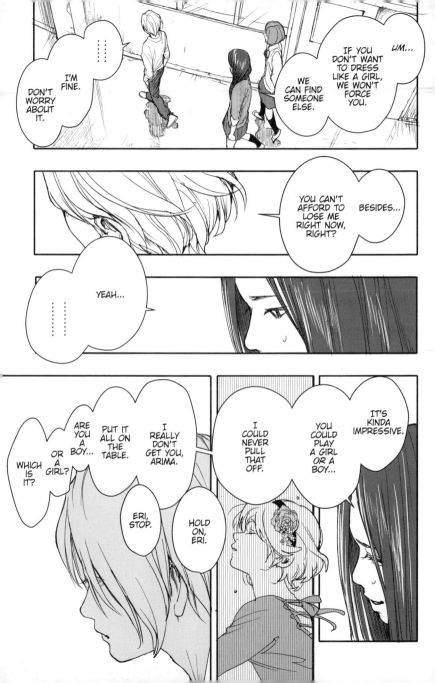

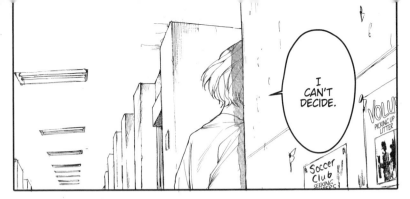

I CAN'T DECIDE.

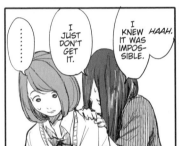

......

I JUST DON'T GET IT.

I KNEW IT WAS IMPOSSIBLE.

HAAH.

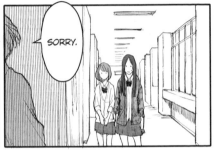

SORRY.

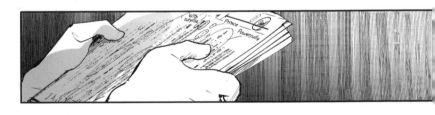

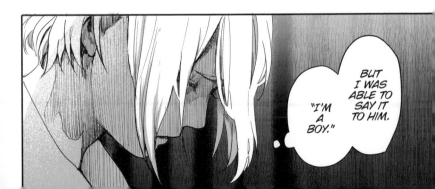

BUT I WAS ABLE TO SAY IT TO HIM.

"I'M A BOY."

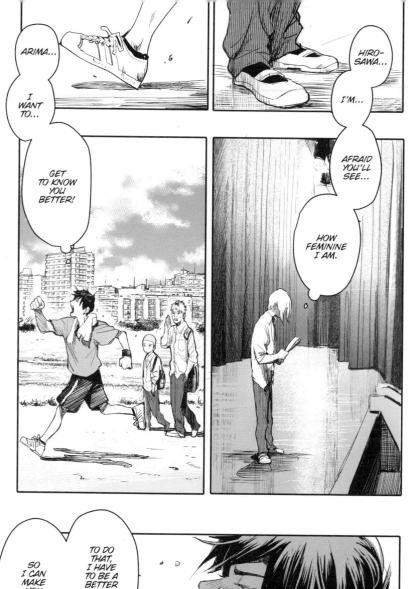

ARIMA...

I WANT TO...

GET TO KNOW YOU BETTER!

HIRO-SAWA...

I'M...

AFRAID YOU'LL SEE...

HOW FEMININE I AM.

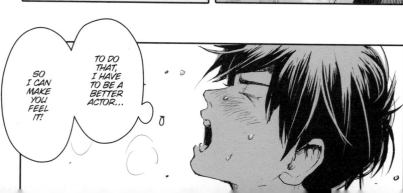

SO I CAN MAKE YOU FEEL IT!

TO DO THAT, I HAVE TO BE A BETTER ACTOR...

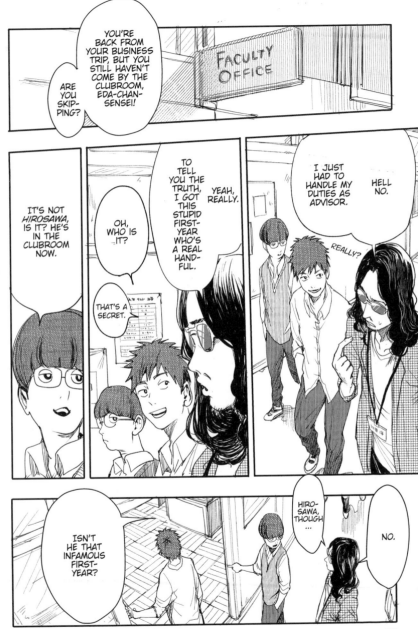

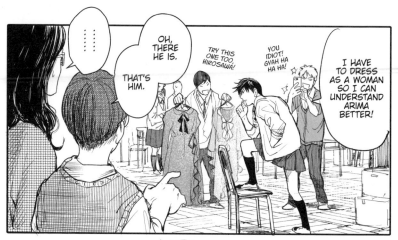

: : :

THAT'S HIM.

OH, THERE HE IS.

TRY THIS ONE TOO, HIROSAWA!

YOU IDIOT! GYAH HA HA HA!

I HAVE TO DRESS AS A WOMAN SO I CAN UNDERSTAND ARIMA BETTER!

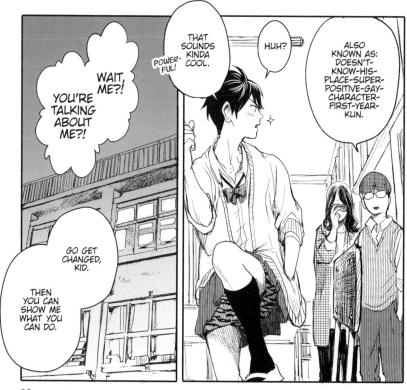

POWER-FUL!

THAT SOUNDS KINDA COOL.

HUH?

ALSO KNOWN AS: DOESN'T-KNOW-HIS-PLACE-SUPER-POSITIVE-GAY-CHARACTER-FIRST-YEAR-KUN.

WAIT, ME?! YOU'RE TALKING ABOUT ME?!

GO GET CHANGED, KID.

THEN YOU CAN SHOW ME WHAT YOU CAN DO.

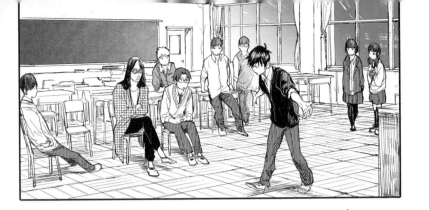

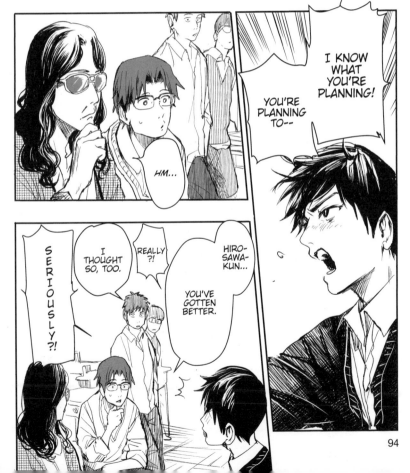

I KNOW WHAT YOU'RE PLANNING!

YOU'RE PLANNING TO--

HM...

SERIOUSLY?!

I THOUGHT SO, TOO.

REALLY?!

HIRO-SAWA-KUN...

YOU'VE GOTTEN BETTER.

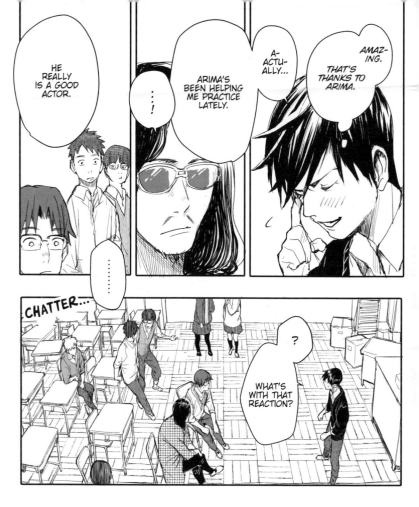

HE REALLY IS A GOOD ACTOR.

......!

ARIMA'S BEEN HELPING ME PRACTICE LATELY.

A-ACTU-ALLY...

AMAZ-ING.

THAT'S THANKS TO ARIMA.

....

CHATTER....

?

WHAT'S WITH THAT REACTION?

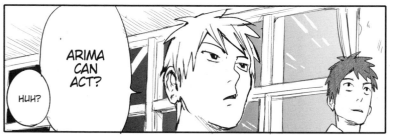

ARIMA CAN ACT?

HUH?

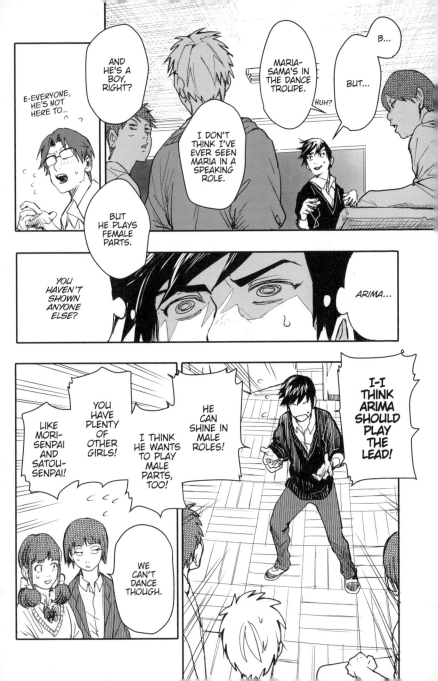

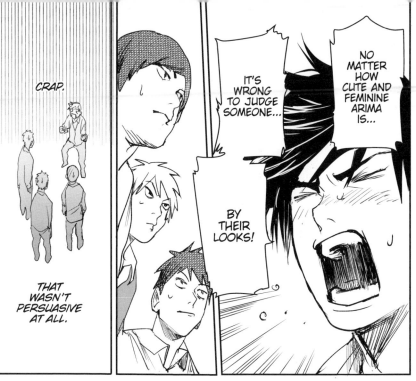

CRAP.

THAT WASN'T PERSUASIVE AT ALL.

IT'S WRONG TO JUDGE SOMEONE...

NO MATTER HOW CUTE AND FEMININE ARIMA IS...

BY THEIR LOOKS!

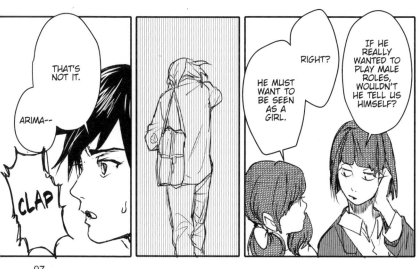

THAT'S NOT IT.

ARIMA--

CLAP

HE MUST WANT TO BE SEEN AS A GIRL.

RIGHT?

IF HE REALLY WANTED TO PLAY MALE ROLES, WOULDN'T HE TELL US HIMSELF?

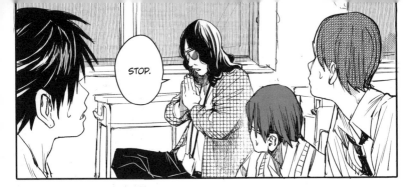

STOP.

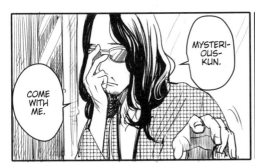

MYSTERI-OUS-KUN.

COME WITH ME.

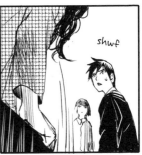

shwf

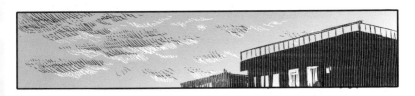

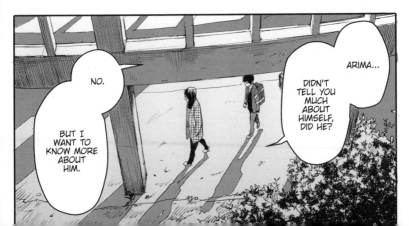

NO.

BUT I WANT TO KNOW MORE ABOUT HIM.

ARIMA...

DIDN'T TELL YOU MUCH ABOUT HIMSELF, DID HE?

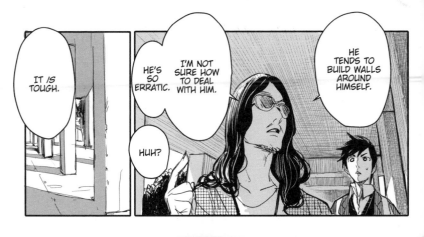

IT *IS* TOUGH.

HE'S SO ERRATIC.

I'M NOT SURE HOW TO DEAL WITH HIM.

HUH?

HE TENDS TO BUILD WALLS AROUND HIMSELF.

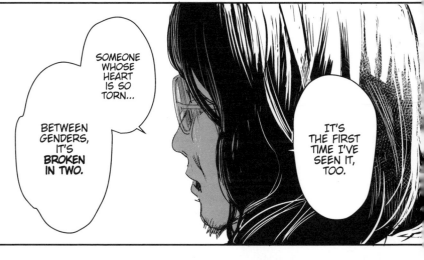

SOMEONE WHOSE HEART IS SO TORN...

BETWEEN GENDERS, IT'S **BROKEN IN TWO.**

IT'S THE FIRST TIME I'VE SEEN IT, TOO.

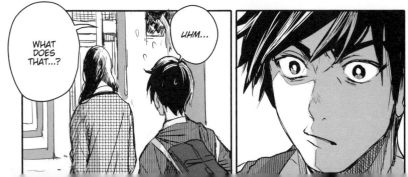

WHAT DOES THAT...?

UHM...

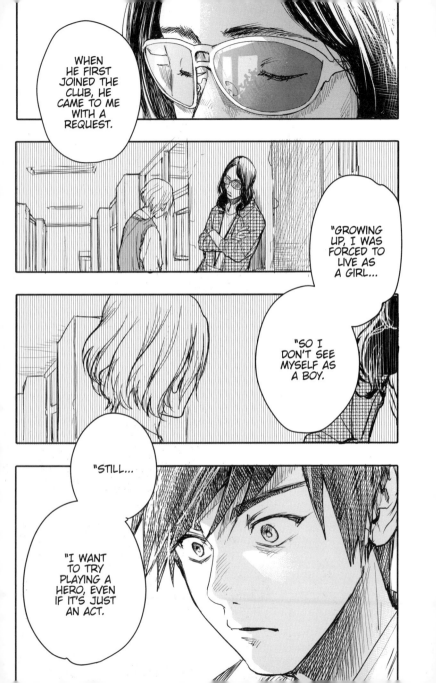

WHEN HE FIRST JOINED THE CLUB, HE CAME TO ME WITH A REQUEST.

"GROWING UP, I WAS FORCED TO LIVE AS A GIRL...

"SO I DON'T SEE MYSELF AS A BOY.

"STILL...

"I WANT TO TRY PLAYING A HERO, EVEN IF IT'S JUST AN ACT.

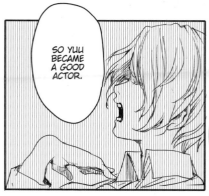

SO YUU BECAME A GOOD ACTOR.

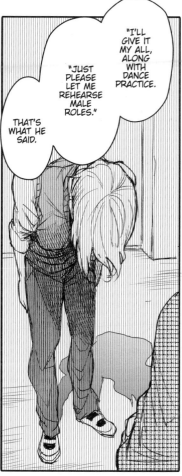

"I'LL GIVE IT MY ALL, ALONG WITH DANCE PRACTICE."

"JUST PLEASE LET ME REHEARSE MALE ROLES."

THAT'S WHAT HE SAID.

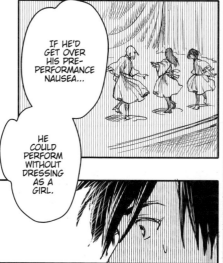

IF HE'D GET OVER HIS PRE-PERFORMANCE NAUSEA...

HE COULD PERFORM WITHOUT DRESSING AS A GIRL.

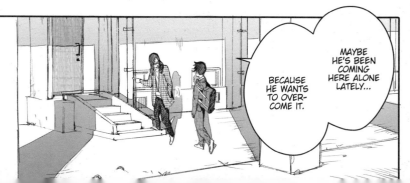

MAYBE HE'S BEEN COMING HERE ALONE LATELY...

BECAUSE HE WANTS TO OVER-COME IT.

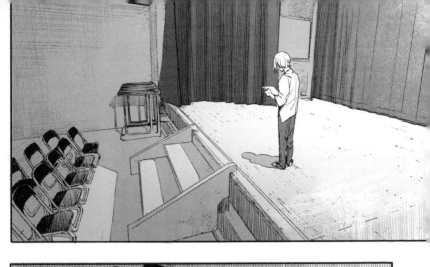

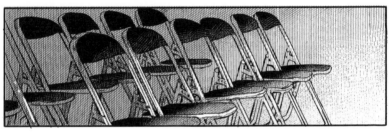

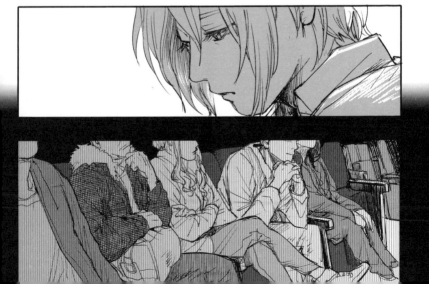

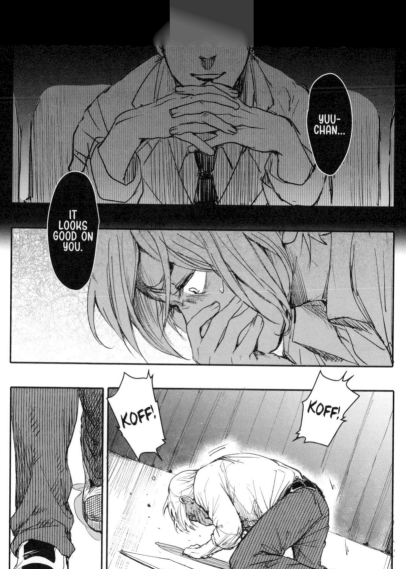
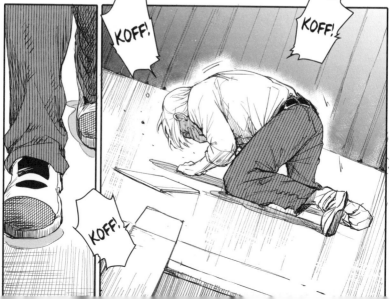

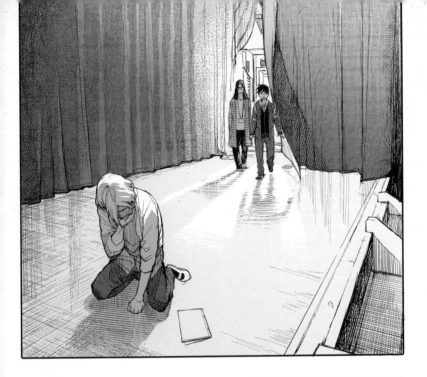

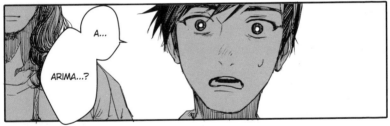

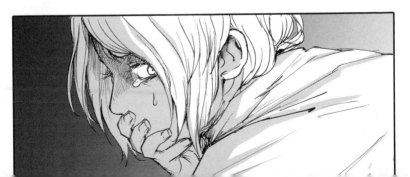

A...

ARIMA...?

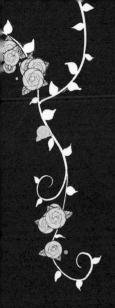

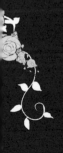

Boy Meets Maria

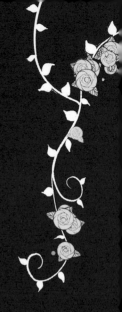

Boy Meets Maria

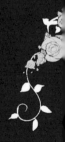

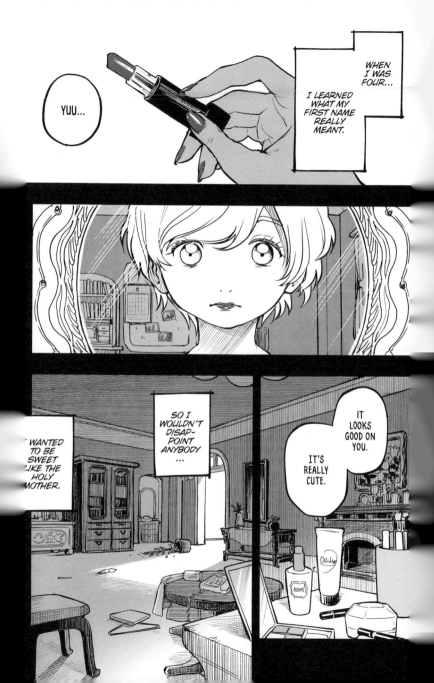

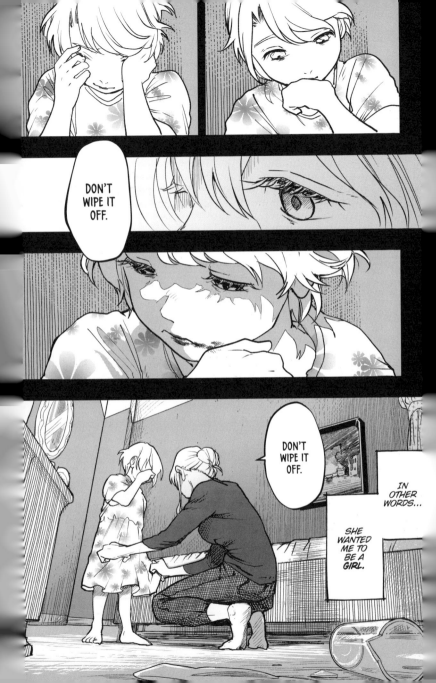

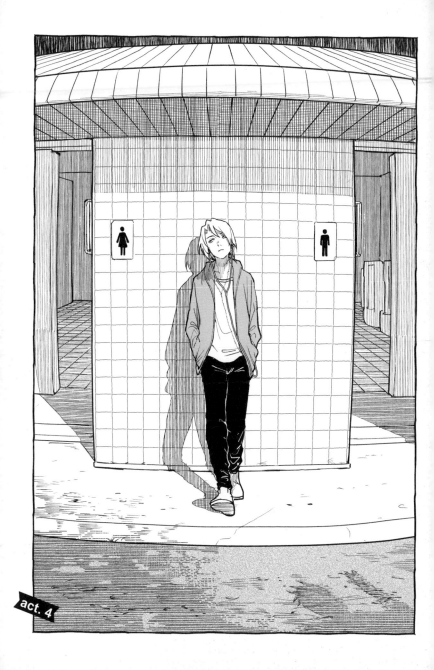

act. 4

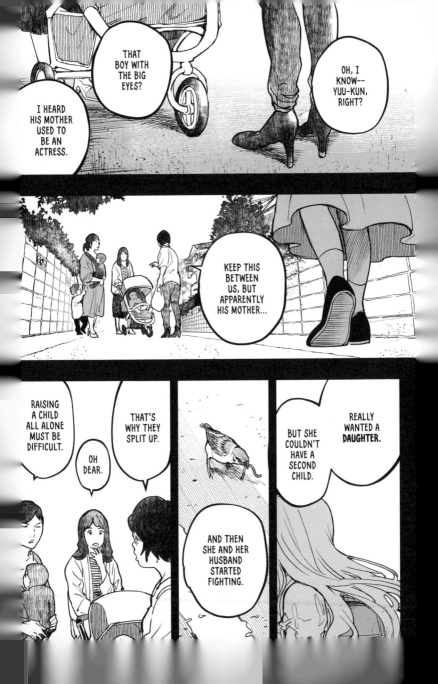

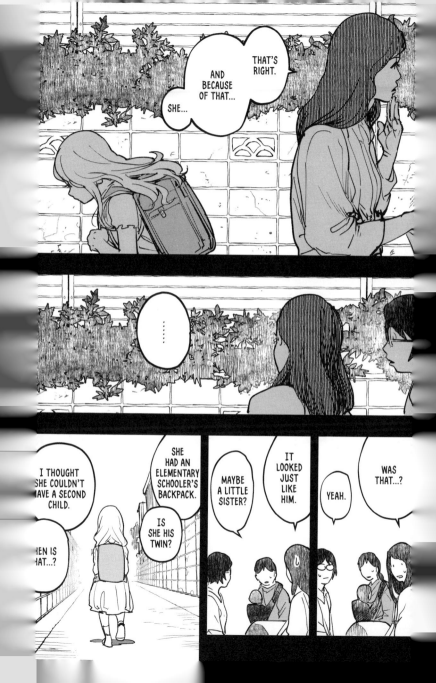

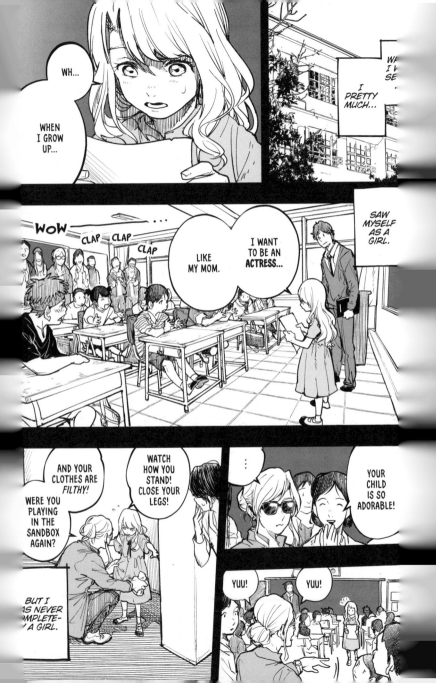

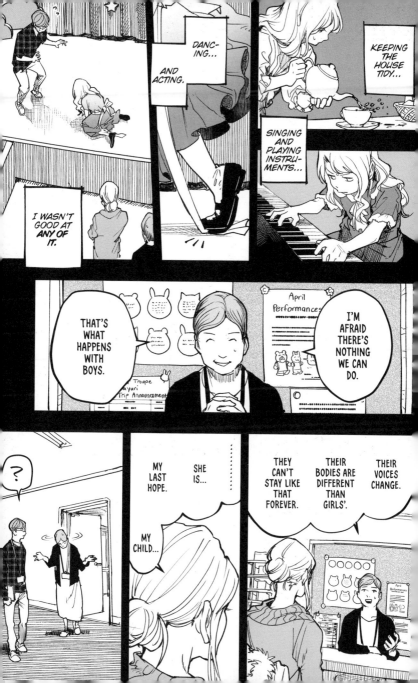

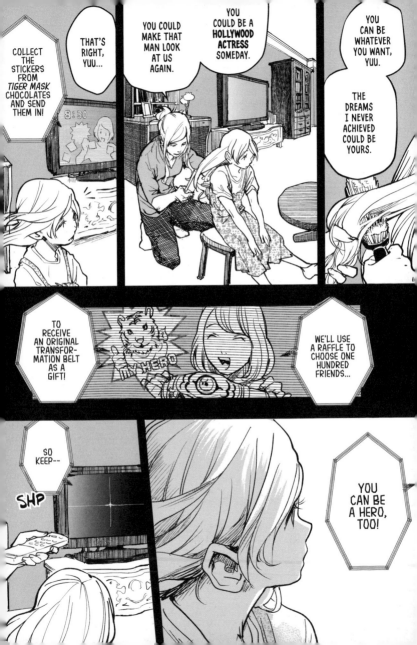

COLLECT THE STICKERS FROM *TIGER MASK* CHOCOLATES AND SEND THEM IN!

THAT'S RIGHT, YUU...

YOU COULD MAKE THAT MAN LOOK AT US AGAIN.

YOU COULD BE A **HOLLYWOOD ACTRESS** SOMEDAY.

YOU CAN BE WHATEVER YOU WANT, YUU.

THE DREAMS I NEVER ACHIEVED COULD BE YOURS.

TO RECEIVE AN ORIGINAL TRANSFORMATION BELT AS A GIFT!

WE'LL USE A RAFFLE TO CHOOSE ONE HUNDRED FRIENDS...

SO KEEP--

SHP

YOU CAN BE A HERO, TOO!

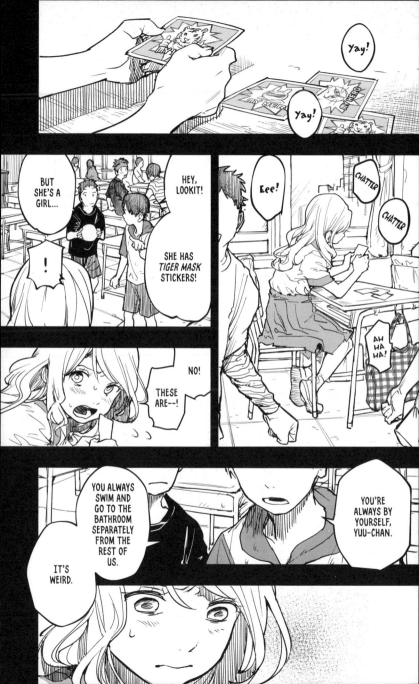

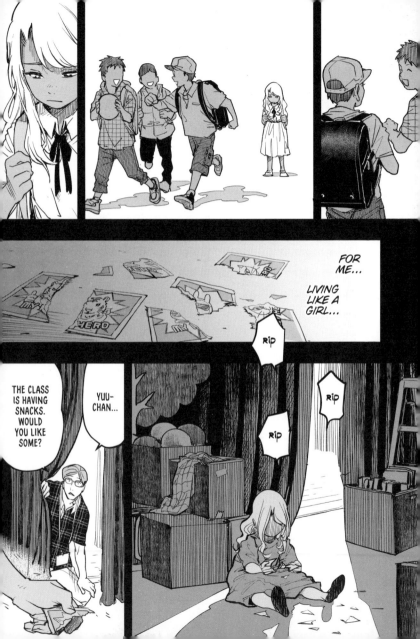

FOR ME...

LIVING LIKE A GIRL...

RIP

THE CLASS IS HAVING SNACKS. WOULD YOU LIKE SOME?

YUU-CHAN...

RIP

RIP

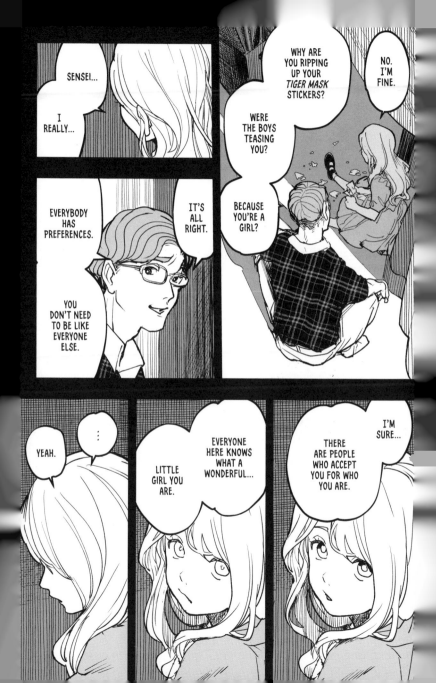

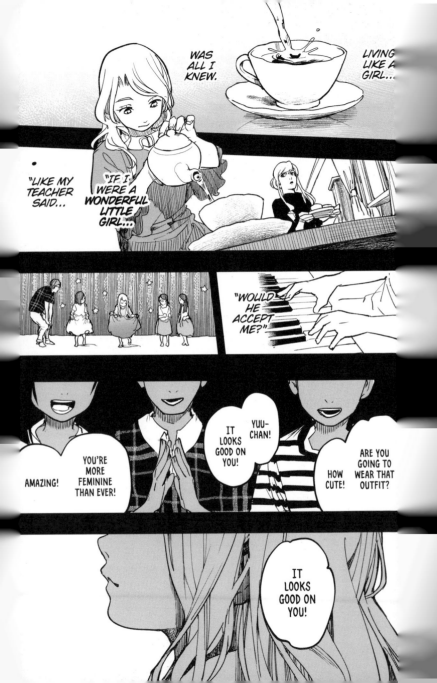

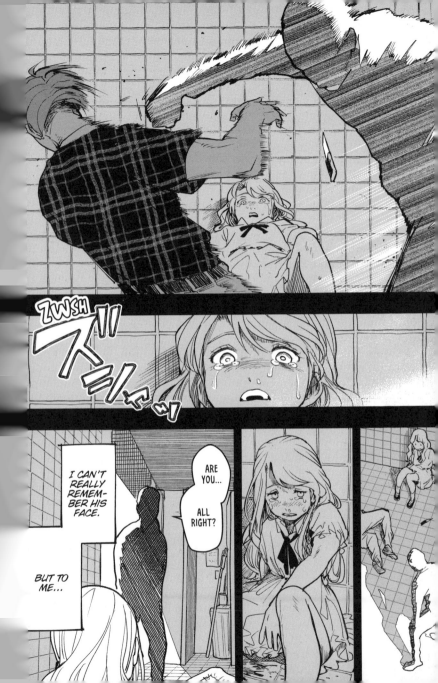

ZWSH

I CAN'T
REALLY
REMEM-
BER HIS
FACE.

BUT TO
ME...

ARE
YOU...

ALL
RIGHT?

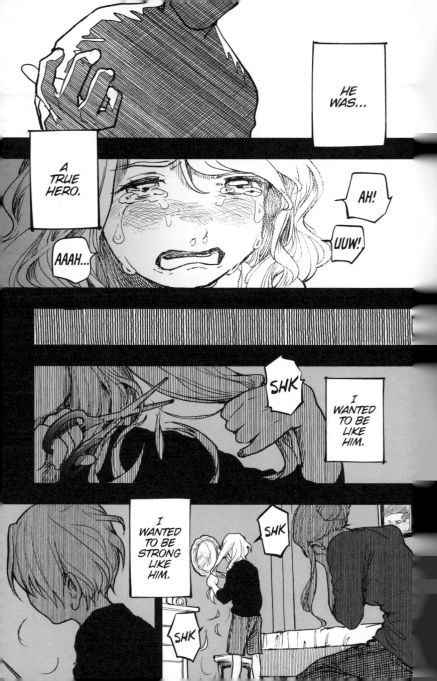

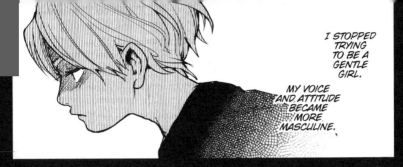

I STOPPED TRYING TO BE A GENTLE GIRL.

MY VOICE AND ATTITUDE BECAME MORE MASCULINE.

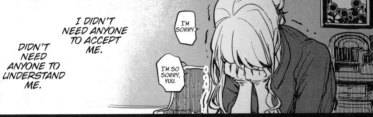

I DIDN'T NEED ANYONE TO ACCEPT ME.

DIDN'T NEED ANYONE TO UNDERSTAND ME.

I'M SORRY.

I'M SO SORRY, YUU.

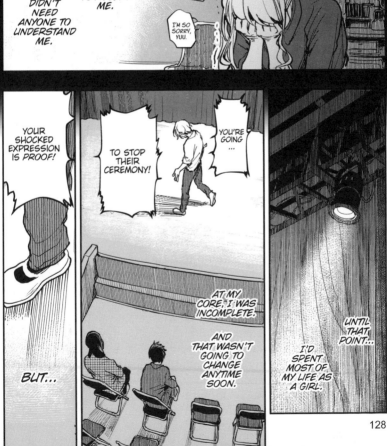

YOUR SHOCKED EXPRESSION IS PROOF!

TO STOP THEIR CEREMONY!

YOU'RE GOING...

AT MY CORE, I WAS INCOMPLETE.

AND THAT WASN'T GOING TO CHANGE ANYTIME SOON.

BUT...

UNTIL THAT POINT...

I'D SPENT MOST OF MY LIFE AS A GIRL.

128

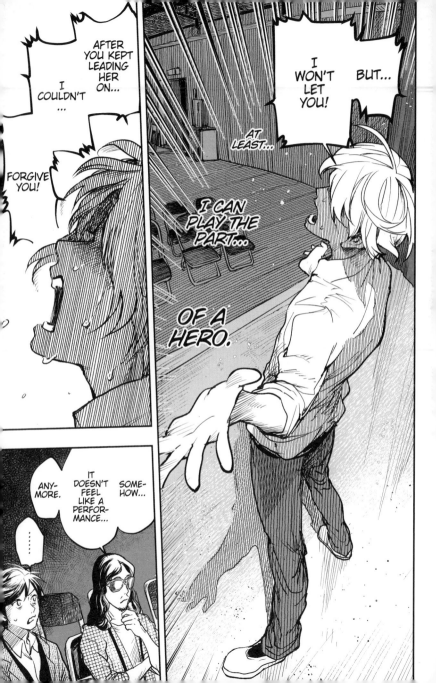

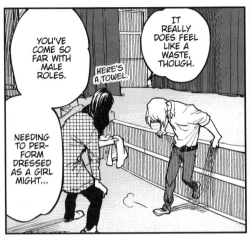

YOU'VE COME SO FAR WITH MALE ROLES.

HERE'S A TOWEL.

IT REALLY DOES FEEL LIKE A WASTE, THOUGH.

NEEDING TO PERFORM DRESSED AS A GIRL MIGHT...

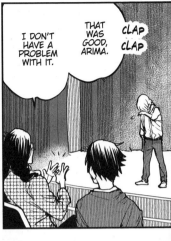

I DON'T HAVE A PROBLEM WITH IT.

THAT WAS GOOD, ARIMA.

CLAP CLAP

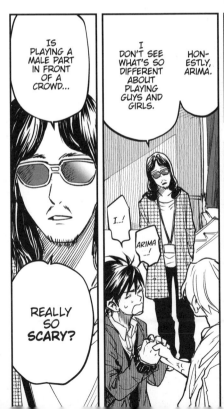

IS PLAYING A MALE PART IN FRONT OF A CROWD...

I DON'T SEE WHAT'S SO DIFFERENT ABOUT PLAYING GUYS AND GIRLS.

HON-ESTLY, ARIMA.

I...!

ARIMA....

REALLY SO SCARY?

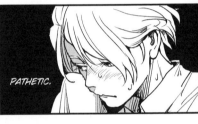

PATHETIC.

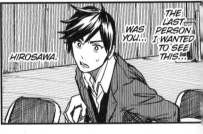

WAS YOU....

THE LAST PERSON I WANTED TO SEE THIS...

HIROSAWA.

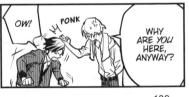

OW!

PONK

WHY ARE *YOU* HERE, ANYWAY?

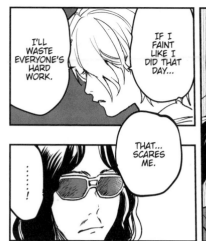

I'LL WASTE EVERYONE'S HARD WORK.

IF I FAINT LIKE I DID THAT DAY...

......!

THAT... SCARES ME.

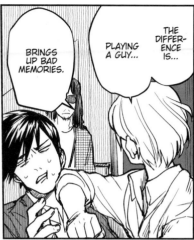

BRINGS UP BAD MEMORIES.

PLAYING A GUY...

THE DIFFERENCE IS...

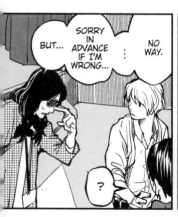

BUT...

SORRY IN ADVANCE IF I'M WRONG...

......

NO WAY.

?

...

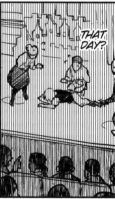

THAT DAY?

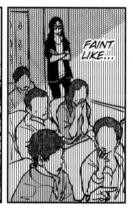

FAINT LIKE...

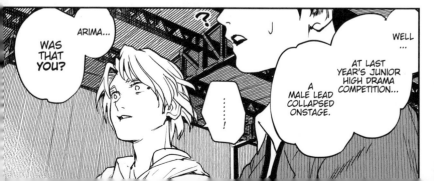

ARIMA...

WAS THAT YOU?

......!

?

J

WELL...

AT LAST YEAR'S JUNIOR HIGH DRAMA COMPETITION...

A MALE LEAD COLLAPSED ONSTAGE.

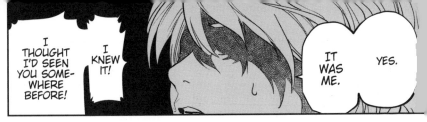

I THOUGHT I'D SEEN YOU SOME- WHERE BEFORE!

I KNEW IT!

IT WAS ME.

YES.

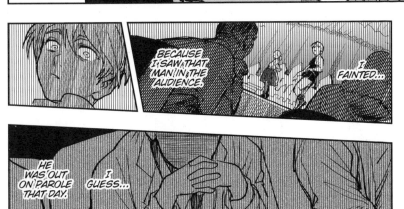

BECAUSE I SAW THAT MAN IN THE AUDIENCE.

I FAINTED...

HE WAS OUT ON PAROLE THAT DAY.

I GUESS...

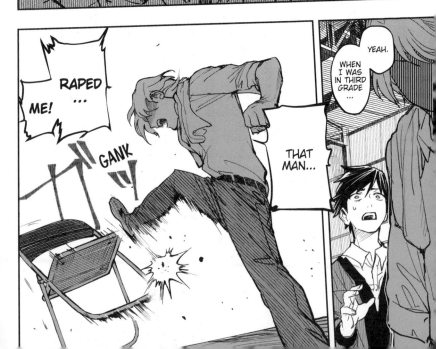

RAPED ...

ME!

GANK

YEAH.

WHEN I WAS IN THIRD GRADE...

THAT MAN...

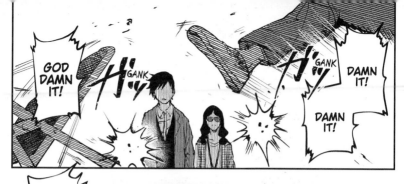

GOD DAMN IT!

H'GANK

H'GANK

DAMN IT!

DAMN IT!

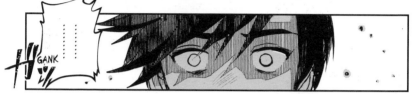

H'GANK

: : : : : :

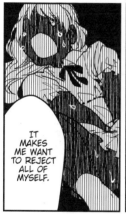

IT MAKES ME WANT TO REJECT ALL OF MYSELF.

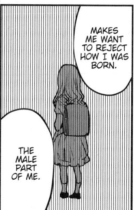

MAKES ME WANT TO REJECT HOW I WAS BORN.

THE MALE PART OF ME.

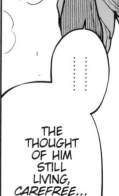

: : :

THE THOUGHT OF HIM STILL LIVING, CAREFREE...

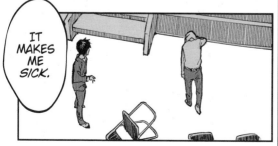

IT MAKES ME SICK.

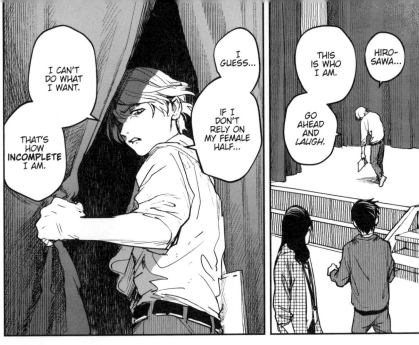

I CAN'T DO WHAT I WANT.

THAT'S HOW INCOMPLETE I AM.

I GUESS...

IF I DON'T RELY ON MY FEMALE HALF...

THIS IS WHO I AM.

GO AHEAD AND LAUGH.

HIRO-SAWA...

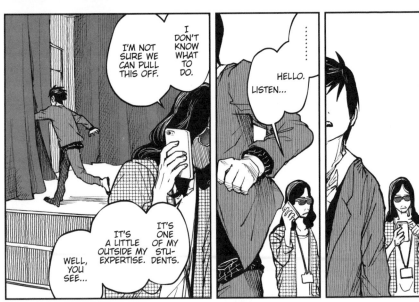

I'M NOT SURE WE CAN PULL THIS OFF.

I DON'T KNOW WHAT TO DO.

············ HELLO. LISTEN...

WELL, YOU SEE... IT'S A LITTLE OUTSIDE MY EXPERTISE. IT'S ONE OF MY STU- DENTS.

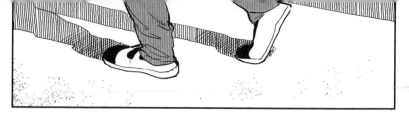

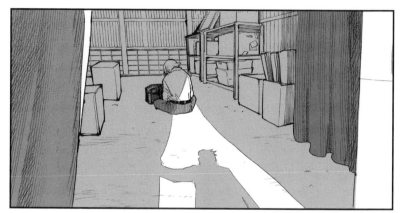

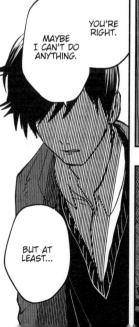

YOU'RE RIGHT.

MAYBE I CAN'T DO ANYTHING.

DON'T WASTE YOUR TIME.

YOU ALWAYS COME AFTER ME.

BUT AT LEAST...

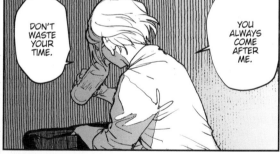

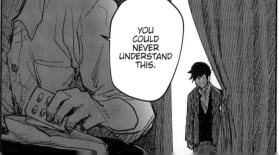

YOU COULD NEVER UNDERSTAND THIS.

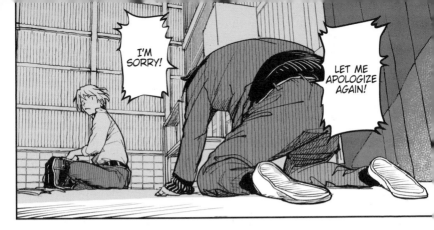

I'M SORRY!

LET ME APOLOGIZE AGAIN!

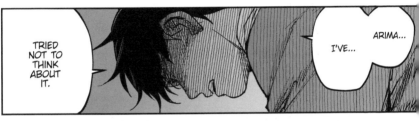

ARIMA...

I'VE...

TRIED NOT TO THINK ABOUT IT.

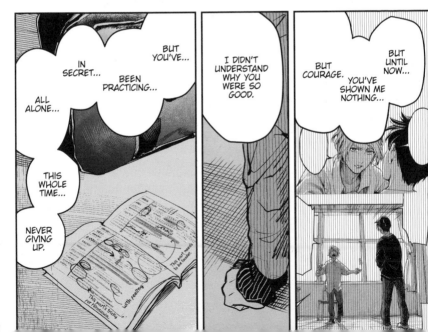

ALL ALONE...

IN SECRET...

BEEN PRACTICING...

BUT YOU'VE...

THIS WHOLE TIME...

NEVER GIVING UP.

I DIDN'T UNDERSTAND WHY YOU WERE SO GOOD.

BUT COURAGE. YOU'VE SHOWN ME NOTHING...

BUT UNTIL NOW...

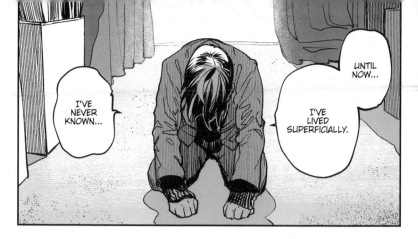

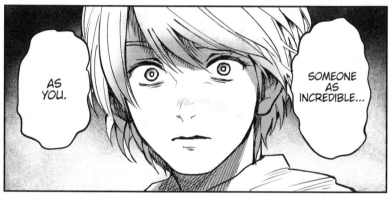

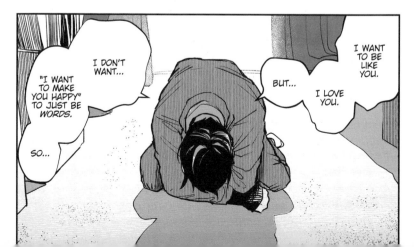

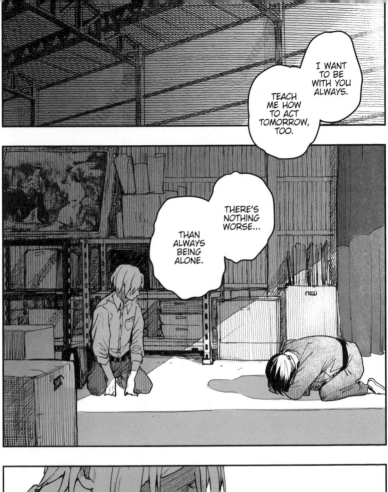

I WANT TO BE WITH YOU ALWAYS.

TEACH ME HOW TO ACT TOMORROW, TOO.

THERE'S NOTHING WORSE...

THAN ALWAYS BEING ALONE.

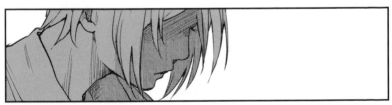

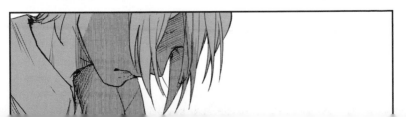

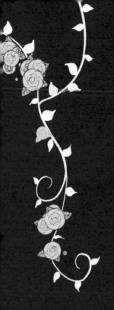

Boy Meets Maria

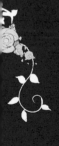

Boy Meets Maria

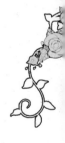

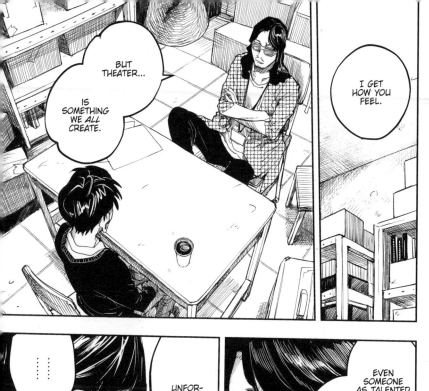

BUT THEATER...

IS SOMETHING WE *ALL* CREATE.

I GET HOW YOU FEEL.

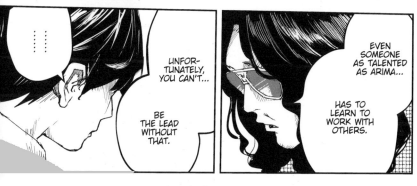

...

UNFORTUNATELY, YOU CAN'T...

BE THE LEAD WITHOUT THAT.

EVEN SOMEONE AS TALENTED AS ARIMA...

HAS TO LEARN TO WORK WITH OTHERS.

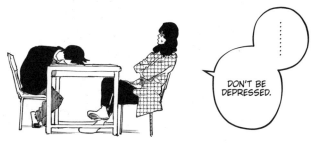

.....

DON'T BE DEPRESSED.

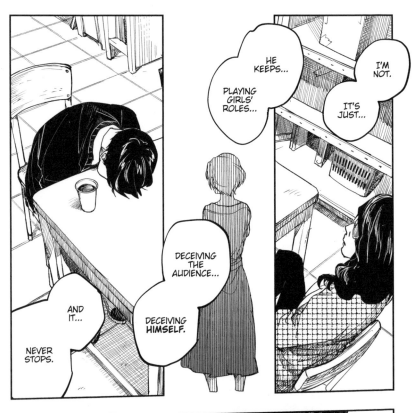

HE KEEPS...

PLAYING GIRLS' ROLES...

I'M NOT.

IT'S JUST...

DECEIVING THE AUDIENCE...

DECEIVING HIMSELF.

AND IT...

NEVER STOPS.

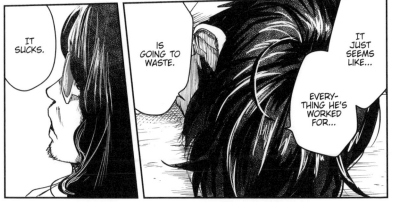

IT SUCKS.

IS GOING TO WASTE.

IT JUST SEEMS LIKE...

EVERY-THING HE'S WORKED FOR...

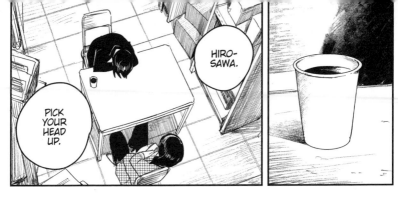

HIRO-SAWA.

PICK YOUR HEAD UP.

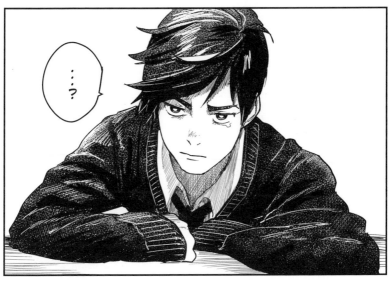

...?

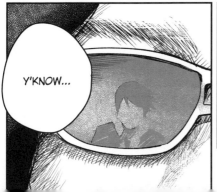

Y'KNOW...

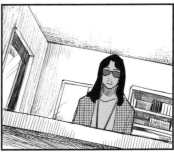

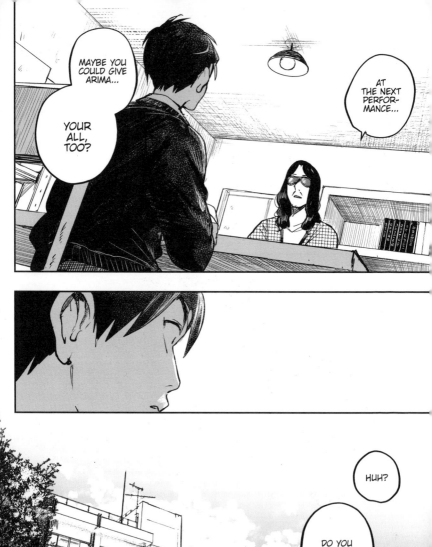

MAYBE YOU COULD GIVE ARIMA...

YOUR ALL, TOO?

AT THE NEXT PERFOR-MANCE...

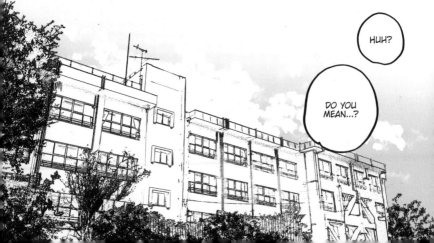

HUH?

DO YOU MEAN...?

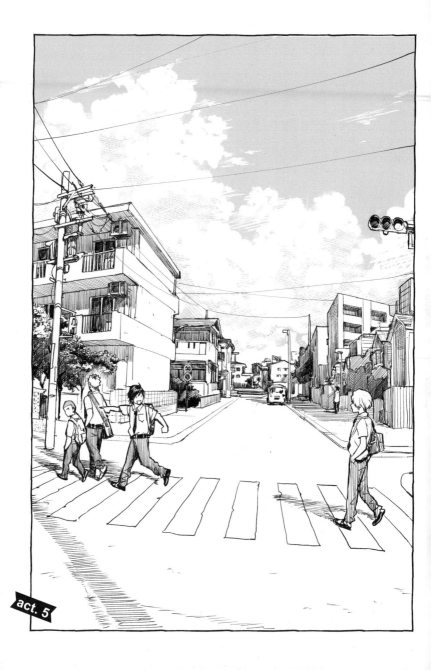

act. 5

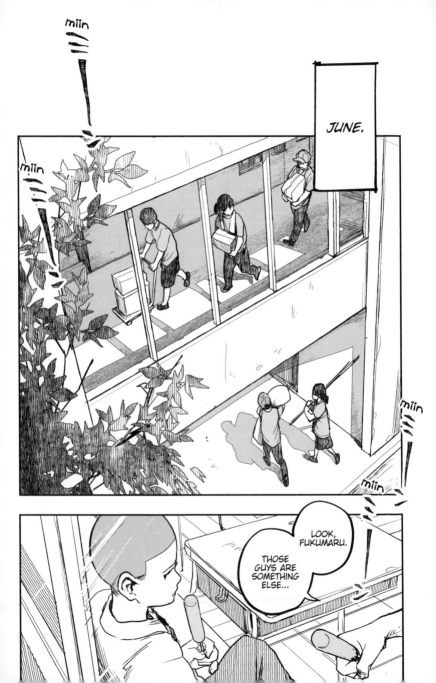

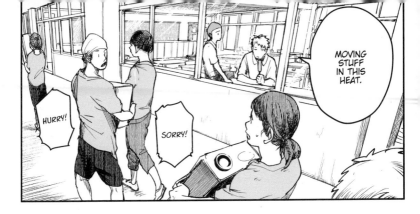

HURRY!

SORRY!

MOVING STUFF IN THIS HEAT.

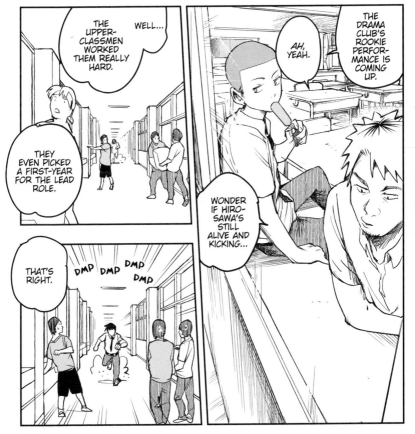

THE UPPERCLASSMEN WORKED THEM REALLY HARD.

WELL...

THEY EVEN PICKED A FIRST-YEAR FOR THE LEAD ROLE.

THAT'S RIGHT.

AH, YEAH.

THE DRAMA CLUB'S ROOKIE PERFORMANCE IS COMING UP.

WONDER IF HIROSAWA'S STILL ALIVE AND KICKING...

DMP
DMP DMP
DMP

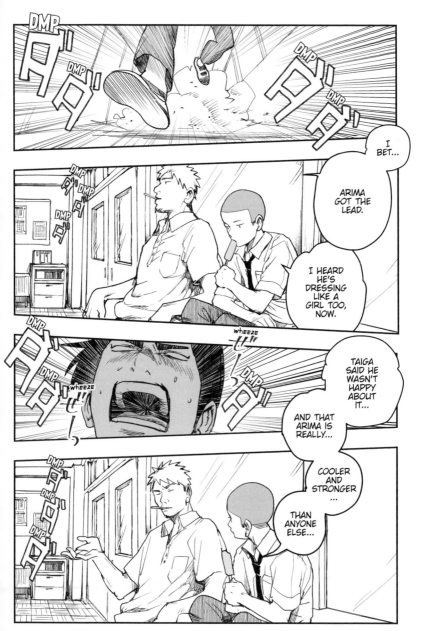

148

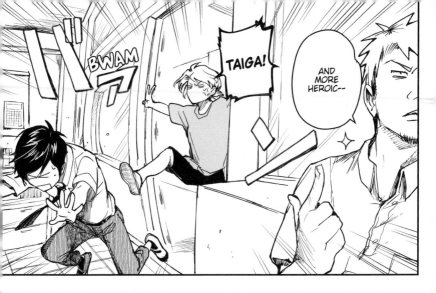

TAIGA!

AND MORE HEROIC--

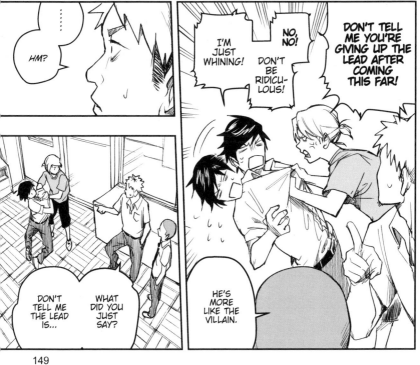

......

HM?

I'M JUST WHINING!

NO, NO! DON'T BE RIDICULOUS!

DON'T TELL ME YOU'RE GIVING UP THE LEAD AFTER COMING THIS FAR!

DON'T TELL ME THE LEAD IS...

WHAT DID YOU JUST SAY?

HE'S MORE LIKE THE VILLAIN.

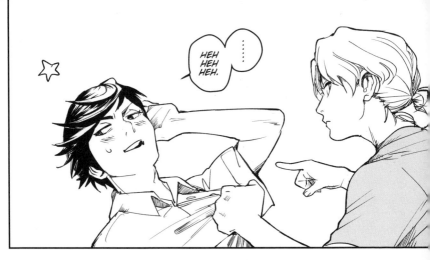

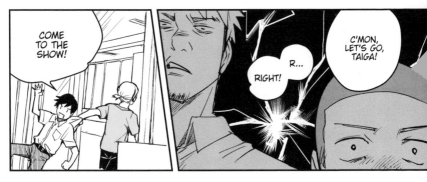

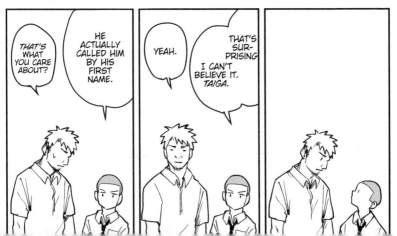

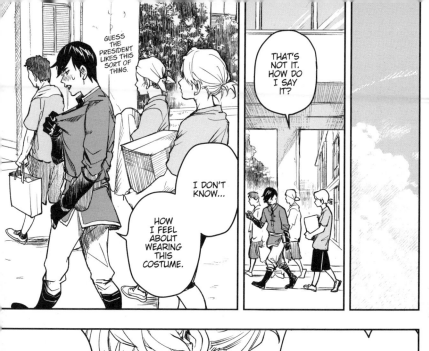

GUESS THE PRESIDENT LIKES THIS SORT OF THING.

THAT'S NOT IT. HOW DO I SAY IT?

I DON'T KNOW...

HOW I FEEL ABOUT WEARING THIS COSTUME.

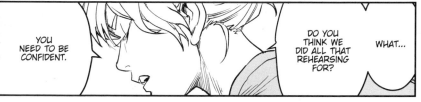

YOU NEED TO BE CONFIDENT.

DO YOU THINK WE DID ALL THAT REHEARSING FOR?

WHAT...

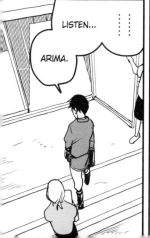

LISTEN...

ARIMA.

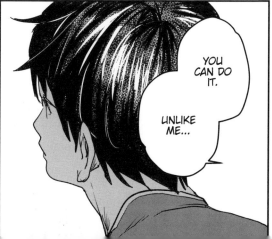

YOU CAN DO IT.

UNLIKE ME...

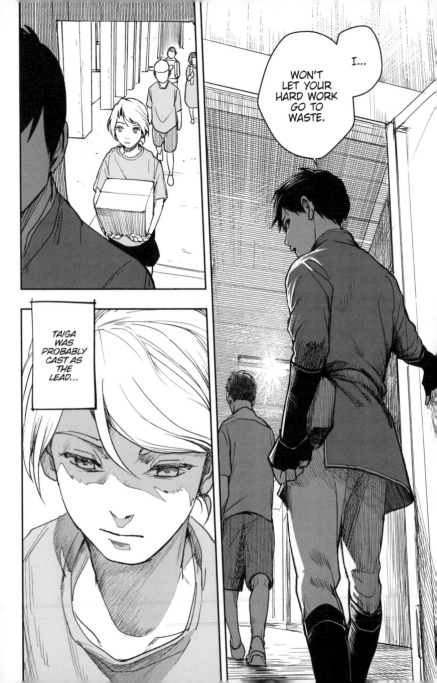

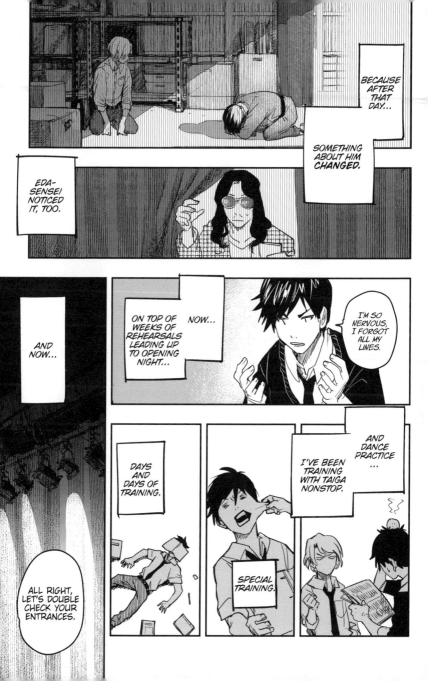

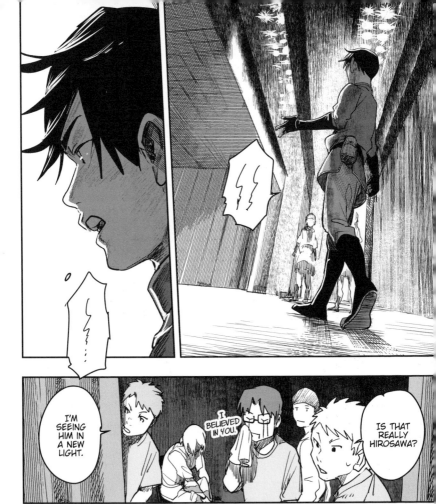

I'M SEEING HIM IN A NEW LIGHT.

I BELIEVED IN YOU.

IS THAT REALLY HIROSAWA?

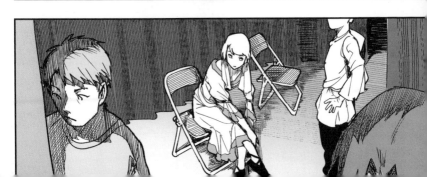

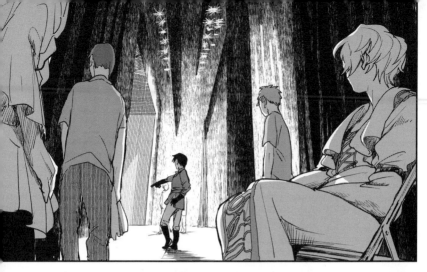

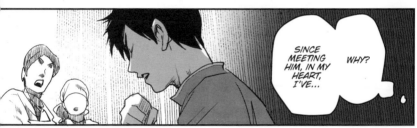

SINCE MEETING HIM, IN MY HEART, I'VE...

WHY?

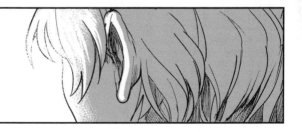

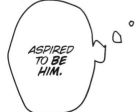

ASPIRED TO BE HIM.

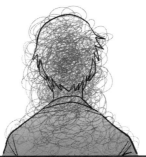

I DON'T KNOW ANYMORE.

WHAT IS HE TO ME?

WHY CAN HE GO PLACES I CAN'T?

WHY IS HE COMFORTABLE WITH THINGS WHEN I'M NOT?

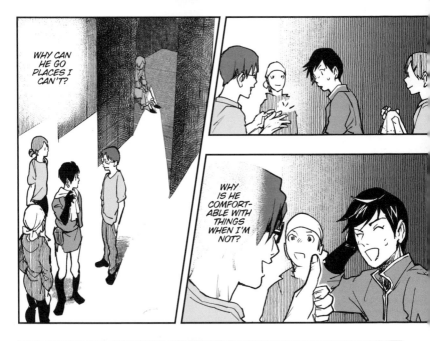

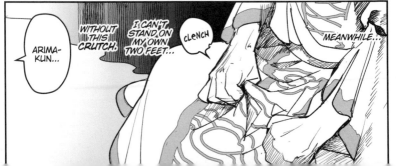

ARIMA-KUN...

WITHOUT THIS CRUTCH.

I CAN'T STAND ON MY OWN TWO FEET...

CLENCH

MEANWHILE...

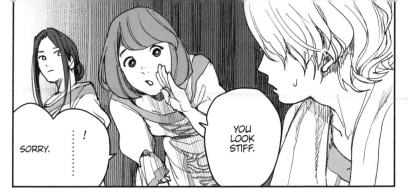

SORRY.

⋯⋯⋯!
⋯⋯⋯

YOU LOOK STIFF.

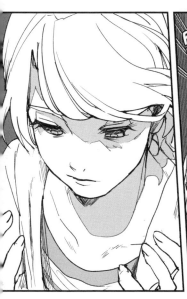

PLAP

I HAVE TO FOCUS ON MYSELF.

RIGHT.

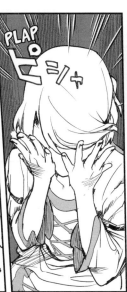

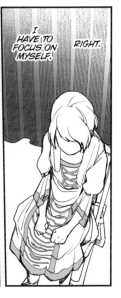

I GOTTA TALK TO YOU.

PRESIDENT.

I HAVE TO FORGET ABOUT THE AUDIENCE.

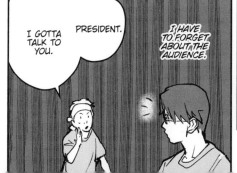

IT'S LIKE HE SWITCHED GENDERS FOR A SECOND.

I'M OKAY WHEN I'M A GIRL.

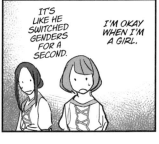

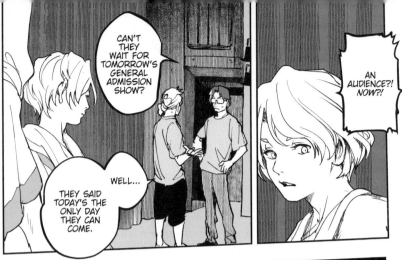

CAN'T THEY WAIT FOR TOMORROW'S GENERAL ADMISSION SHOW?

AN AUDIENCE?! NOW?!

WELL...

THEY SAID TODAY'S THE ONLY DAY THEY CAN COME.

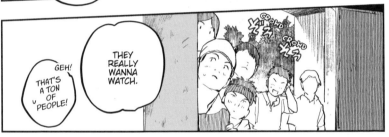

GEH! THAT'S A TON OF PEOPLE!

THEY REALLY WANNA WATCH.

CROWD

CROWD

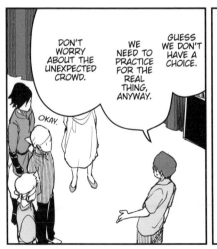

DON'T WORRY ABOUT THE UNEXPECTED CROWD.

WE NEED TO PRACTICE FOR THE REAL THING, ANYWAY.

GUESS WE DON'T HAVE A CHOICE.

OKAY.

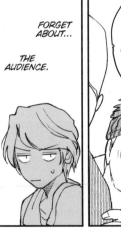

FORGET ABOUT...

THE AUDIENCE.

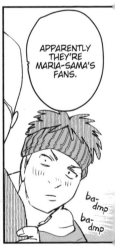

APPARENTLY THEY'RE MARIA-SAMA'S FANS.

ba-dmp

ba-dmp

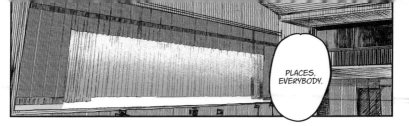

PLACES, EVERYBODY.

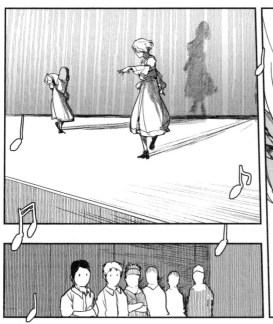

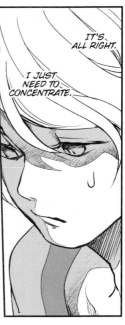

IT'S ALL RIGHT.

I JUST NEED TO CONCENTRATE.

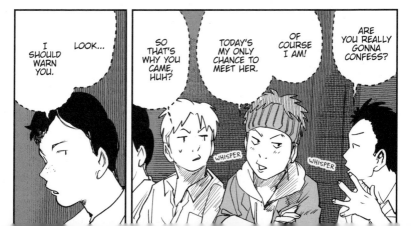

I SHOULD WARN YOU.

LOOK...

SO THAT'S WHY YOU CAME, HUH?

TODAY'S MY ONLY CHANCE TO MEET HER.

OF COURSE I AM!

ARE YOU REALLY GONNA CONFESS?

WHISPER

WHISPER

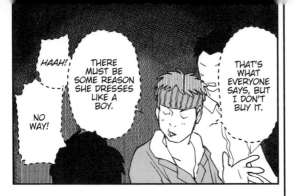

HAAH!

THERE MUST BE SOME REASON SHE DRESSES LIKE A BOY.

NO WAY!

THAT'S WHAT EVERYONE SAYS, BUT I DON'T BUY IT.

YOU'VE SEEN HIM IN HIS SCHOOL UNIFORM, RIGHT?

THAT'S A BOY.

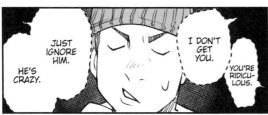

JUST IGNORE HIM.

HE'S CRAZY.

I DON'T GET YOU.

YOU'RE RIDICULOUS.

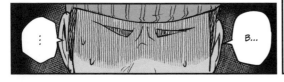

...

B...

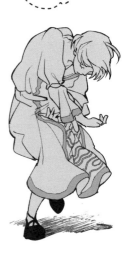

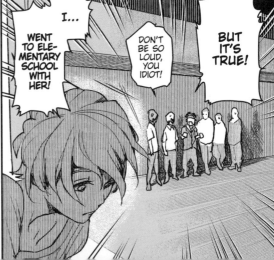

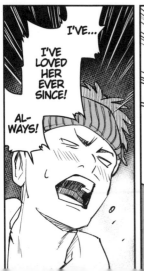

I'VE...

I'VE LOVED HER EVER SINCE!

ALWAYS!

I...

WENT TO ELEMENTARY SCHOOL WITH HER!

DON'T BE SO LOUD, YOU IDIOT!

BUT IT'S TRUE!

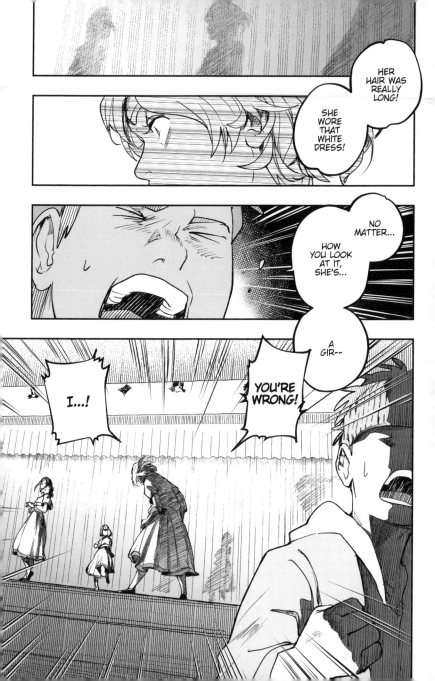

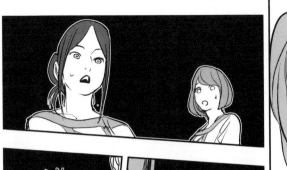

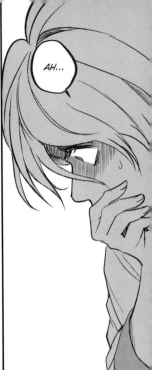

AH...

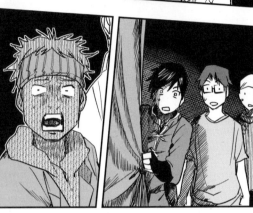

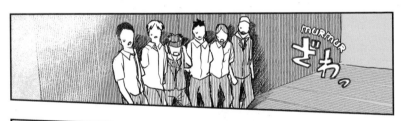

MURMUR

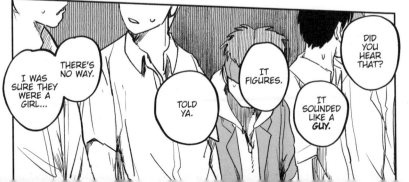

DID YOU HEAR THAT?

IT FIGURES.

IT SOUNDED LIKE A GUY.

THERE'S NO WAY.

TOLD YA.

I WAS SURE THEY WERE A GIRL...

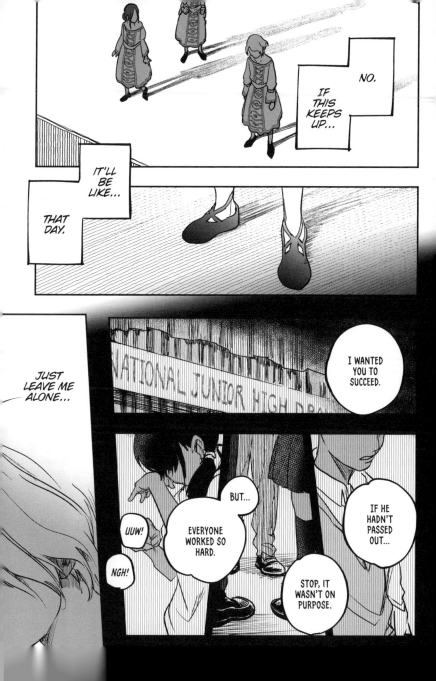

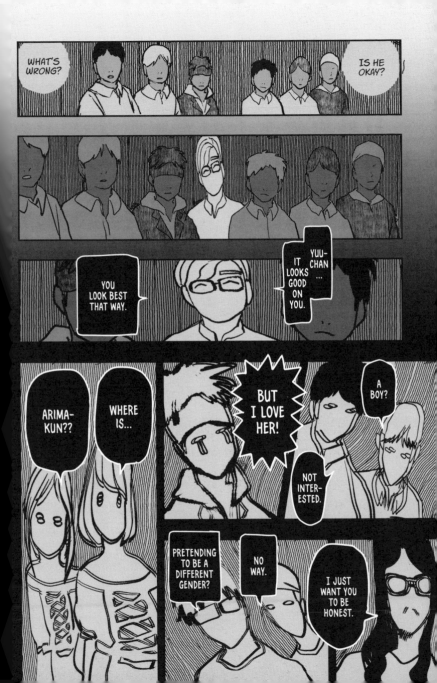

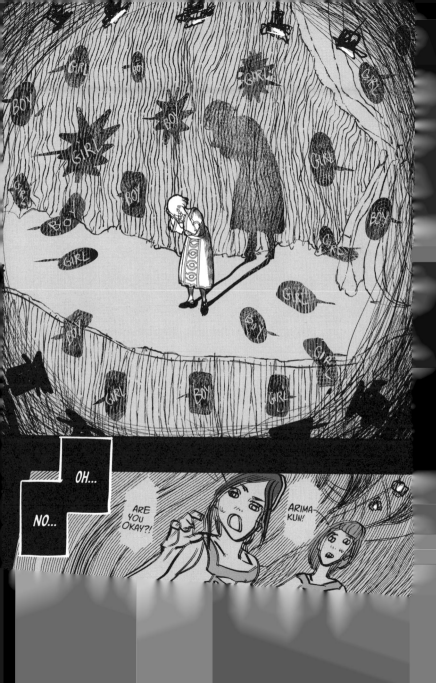

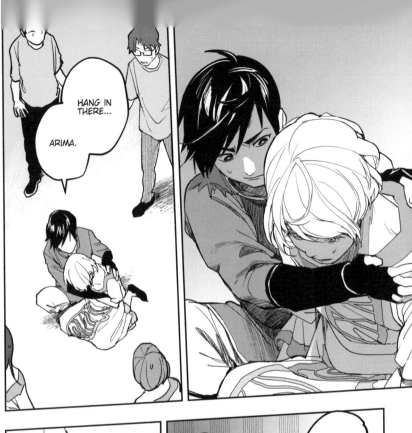

HANG IN THERE...

ARIMA.

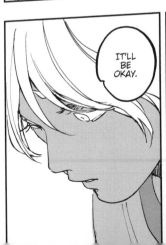

IT'LL BE OKAY.

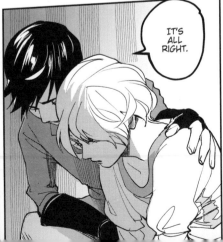

IT'S ALL RIGHT.

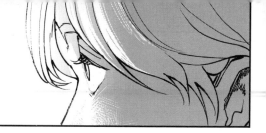

AT THAT
MOMENT, I
UNDERSTOOD...

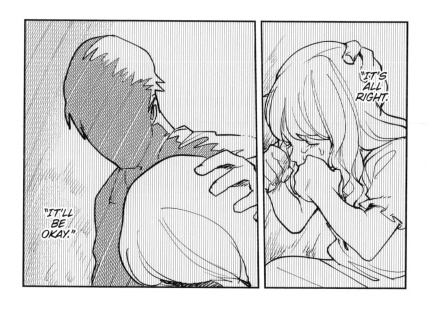

"IT'S
ALL
RIGHT."

"IT'LL
BE
OKAY."

WHY I
FEEL LIKE
THIS ABOUT
YOU...

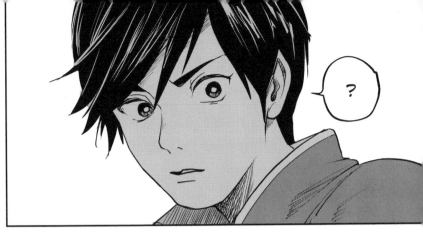

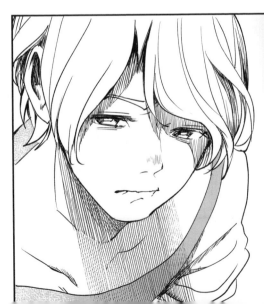

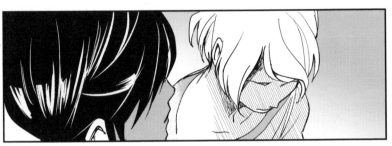

TAIGA...

YOU...

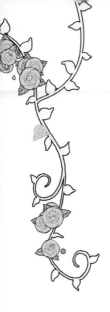

Boy Meets Maria

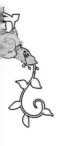

Boy Meets Maria

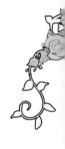

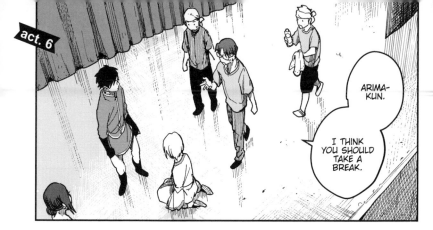

act. 6

ARIMA-KUN.

I THINK YOU SHOULD TAKE A BREAK.

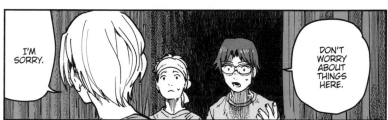

I'M SORRY.

DON'T WORRY ABOUT THINGS HERE.

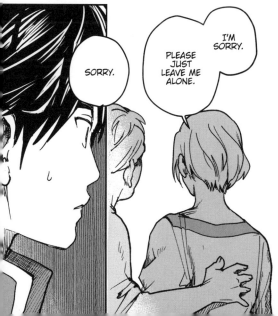

SORRY.

PLEASE JUST LEAVE ME ALONE.

I'M SORRY.

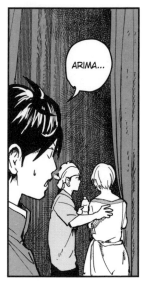

ARIMA...

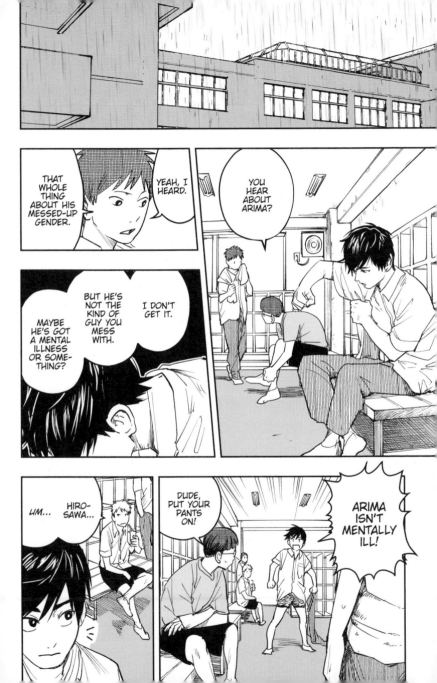

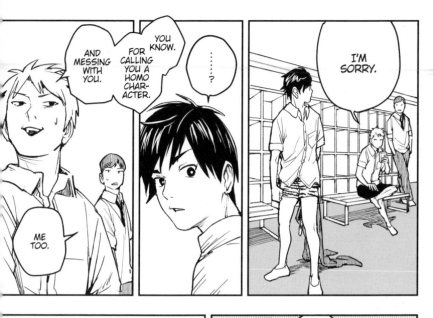

AND MESSING WITH YOU.

FOR CALLING YOU A HOMO CHARACTER.

YOU KNOW.

......?

I'M SORRY.

ME TOO.

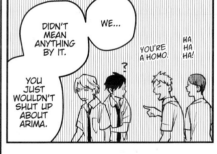

WAIT, SO WHAT'S A HO-WHATEVER?

OKAY...

GA-KNK

DIDN'T MEAN ANYTHING BY IT.

WE...

YOU'RE A HOMO.

HA HA HA!

YOU JUST WOULDN'T SHUT UP ABOUT ARIMA.

......?

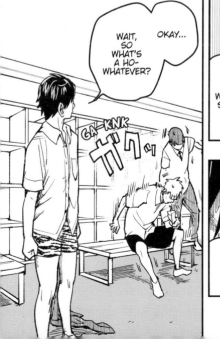

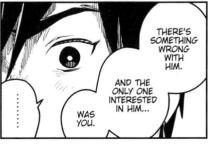

THERE'S SOMETHING WRONG WITH HIM.

AND THE ONLY ONE INTERESTED IN HIM...

....

WAS YOU.

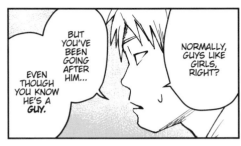

NORMALLY, GUYS LIKE GIRLS, RIGHT?

BUT YOU'VE BEEN GOING AFTER HIM...

EVEN THOUGH YOU KNOW HE'S A **GUY.**

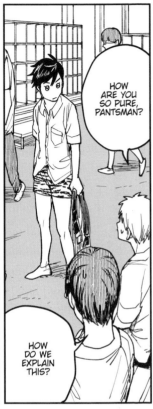

HOW ARE YOU SO PURE, PANTSMAN?

HOW DO WE EXPLAIN THIS?

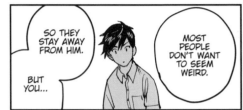

MOST PEOPLE DON'T WANT TO SEEM WEIRD.

SO THEY STAY AWAY FROM HIM.

BUT YOU...

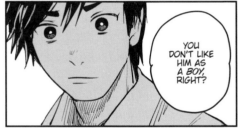

YOU DON'T LIKE HIM AS A *BOY*, RIGHT?

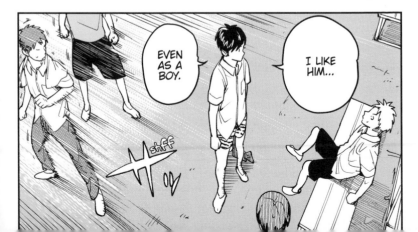

I LIKE HIM...

EVEN AS A BOY.

shff

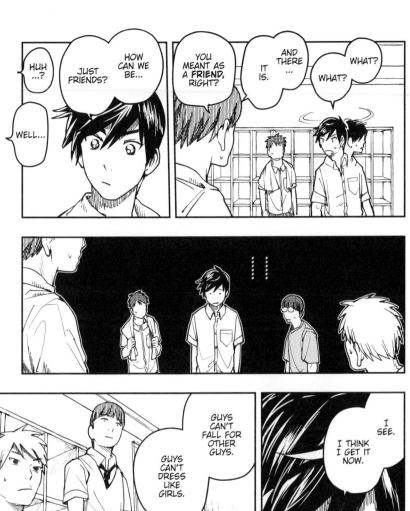

HUH...?

JUST FRIENDS?

HOW CAN WE BE...

YOU MEANT AS A **FRIEND**, RIGHT?

AND THERE...

IT IS.

WHAT?

WHAT?

WELL...

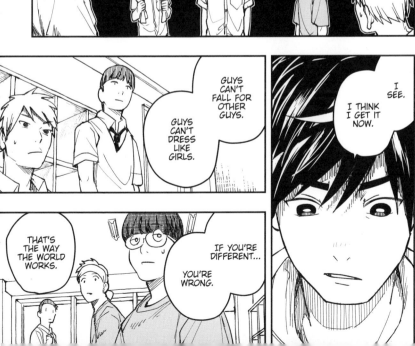

GUYS CAN'T FALL FOR OTHER GUYS.

GUYS CAN'T DRESS LIKE GIRLS.

I SEE. I THINK I GET IT NOW.

THAT'S THE WAY THE WORLD WORKS.

IF YOU'RE DIFFERENT...

YOU'RE WRONG.

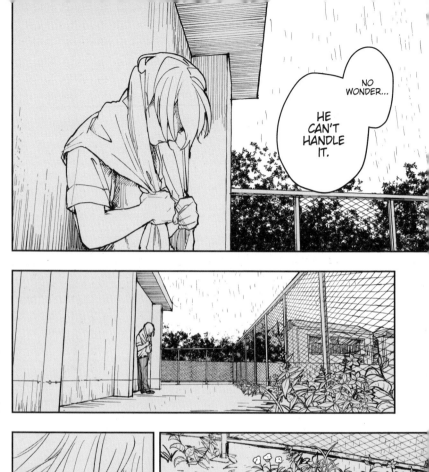

NO WONDER...

HE CAN'T HANDLE IT.

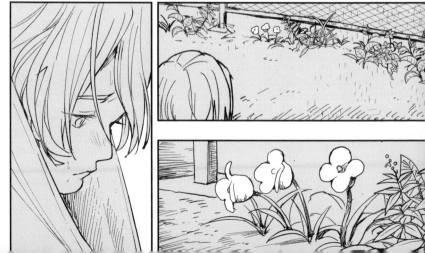

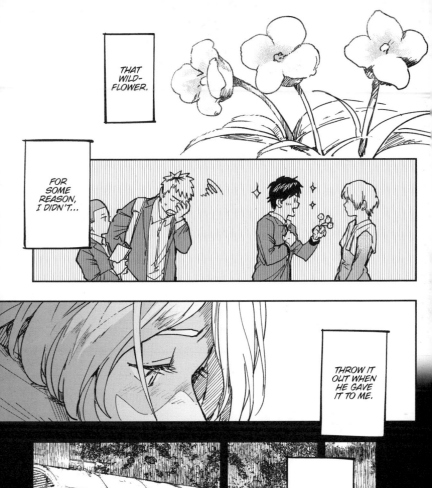

THAT WILD-FLOWER.

FOR SOME REASON, I DIDN'T...

THROW IT OUT WHEN HE GAVE IT TO ME.

NOW I UNDERSTAND WHY.

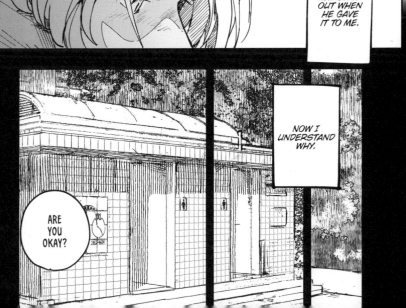

ARE YOU OKAY?

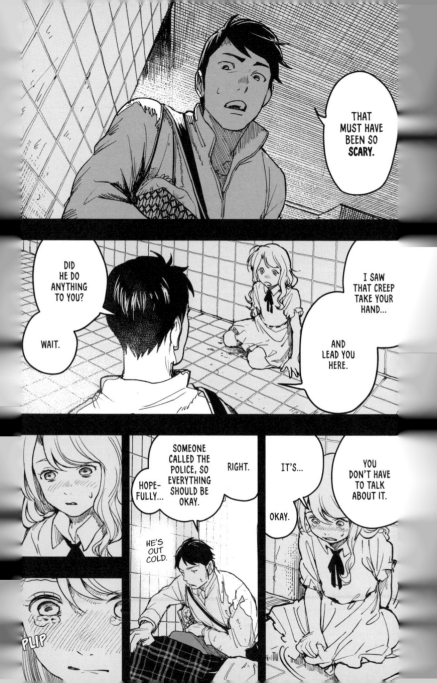

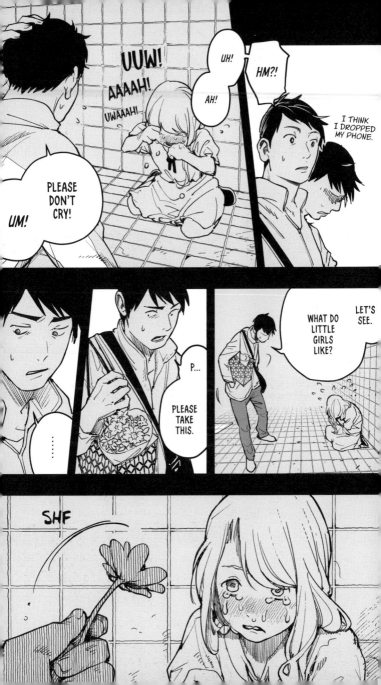

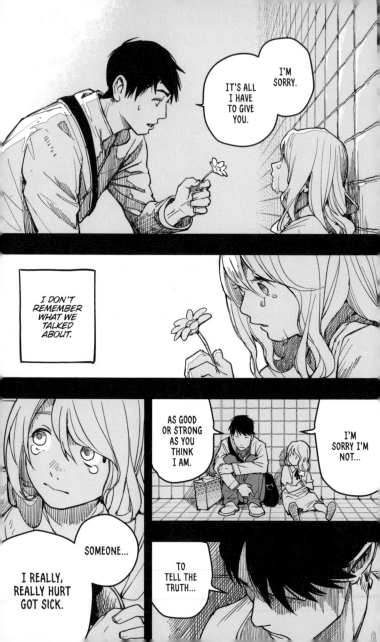

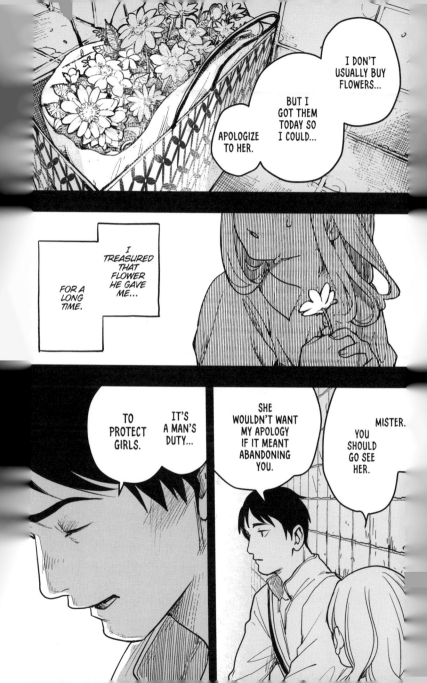

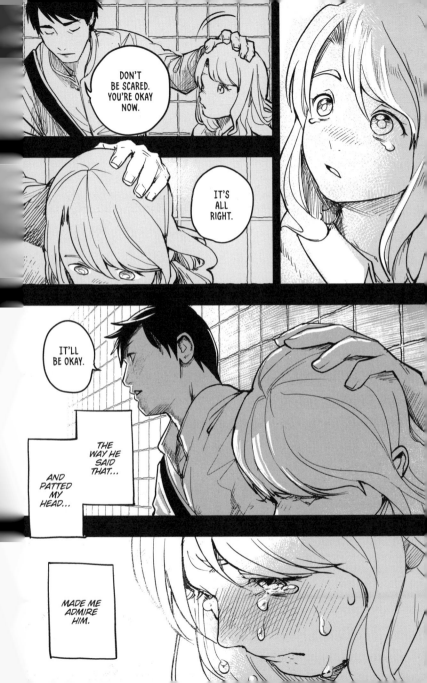

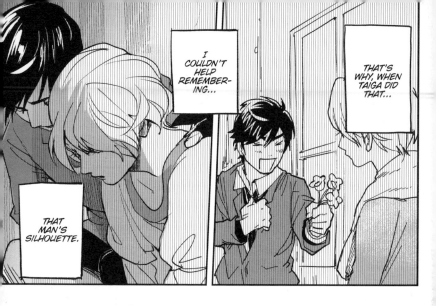

THAT MAN'S SILHOUETTE.

I COULDN'T HELP REMEMBER-ING...

THAT'S WHY, WHEN TAIGA DID THAT...

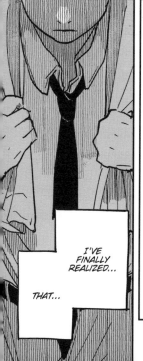

I'VE FINALLY REALIZED...

THAT...

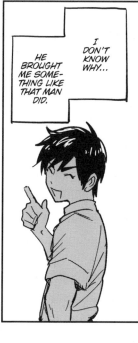

HE BROUGHT ME SOME-THING LIKE THAT MAN DID.

I DON'T KNOW WHY...

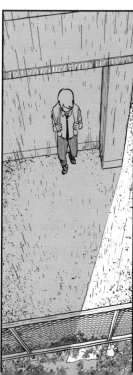

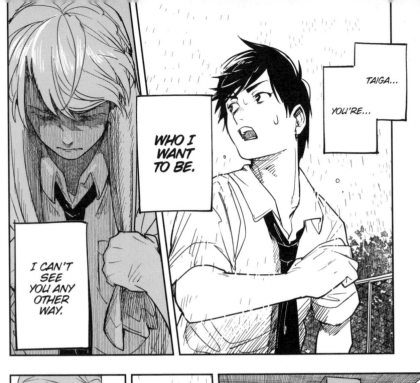

TAIGA...

YOU'RE...

WHO I WANT TO BE.

I CAN'T SEE YOU ANY OTHER WAY.

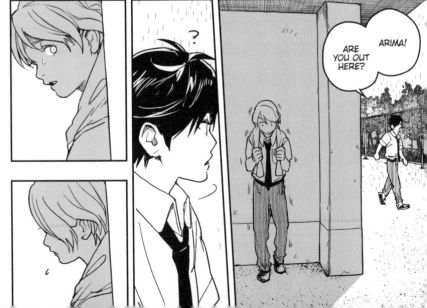

?

ARE YOU OUT HERE?

ARIMA!

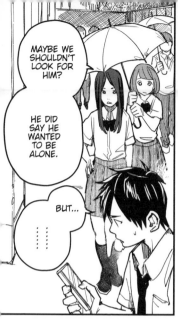

MAYBE WE SHOULDN'T LOOK FOR HIM?

HE DID SAY HE WANTED TO BE ALONE.

BUT...

......

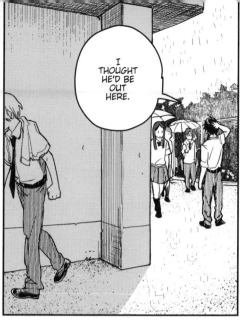

I THOUGHT HE'D BE OUT HERE.

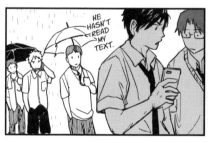

HE HASN'T READ MY TEXT.

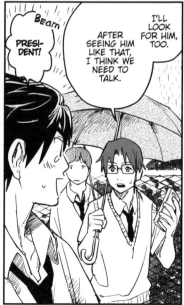

Beam

PRESI-DENT!

AFTER SEEING HIM LIKE THAT, I THINK WE NEED TO TALK.

I'LL LOOK FOR HIM, TOO.

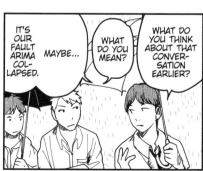

IT'S OUR FAULT ARIMA COLLAPSED.

MAYBE...

WHAT DO YOU MEAN?

WHAT DO YOU THINK ABOUT THAT CONVERSATION EARLIER?

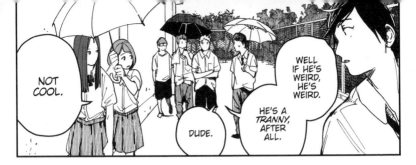

NOT COOL.

DUDE.

HE'S A *TRANNY*, AFTER ALL.

WELL IF HE'S WEIRD, HE'S WEIRD.

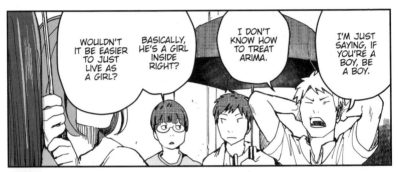

WOULDN'T IT BE EASIER TO JUST LIVE AS A GIRL?

BASICALLY, HE'S A GIRL INSIDE RIGHT?

I DON'T KNOW HOW TO TREAT ARIMA.

I'M JUST SAYING, IF YOU'RE A BOY, BE A BOY.

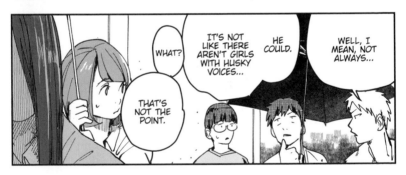

WHAT?

THAT'S NOT THE POINT.

IT'S NOT LIKE THERE AREN'T GIRLS WITH HUSKY VOICES...

HE COULD.

WELL, I MEAN, NOT ALWAYS...

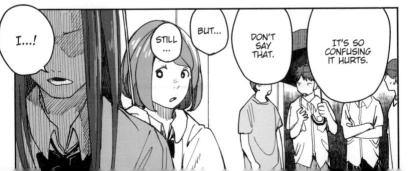

I...!

STILL...

BUT...

DON'T SAY THAT.

IT'S SO CONFUSING IT HURTS.

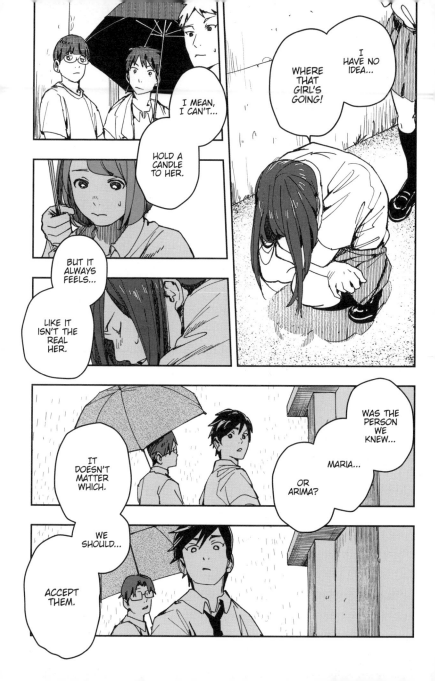

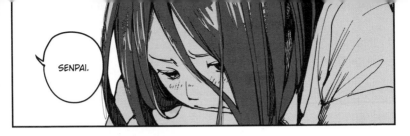

SENPAI.

WHAT?

ARIMA... YOU KNOW...

・・・・

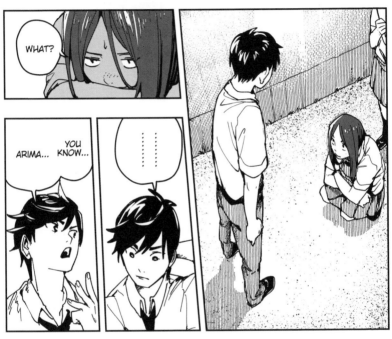

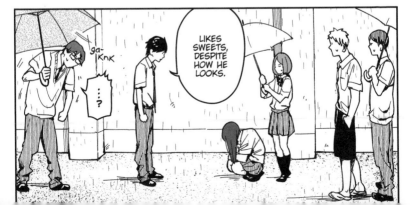

ga-knk

...?

LIKES SWEETS, DESPITE HOW HE LOOKS.

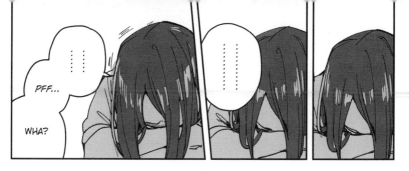

PFF...

WHA?

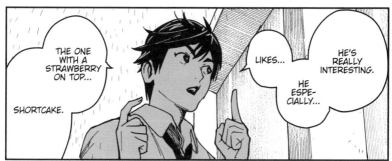

THE ONE WITH A STRAWBERRY ON TOP...

SHORTCAKE.

LIKES...

HE ESPE-CIALLY...

HE'S REALLY INTERESTING.

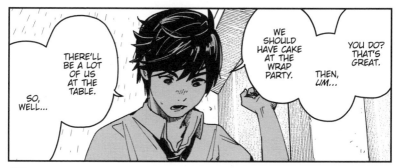

I LIKE SHORTCAKE, TOO.

SO?

SERIOUSLY?

HEH... HEH HEH...

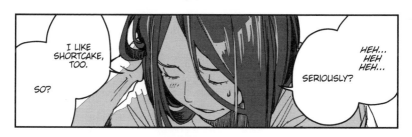

THERE'LL BE A LOT OF US AT THE TABLE.

SO, WELL...

WE SHOULD HAVE CAKE AT THE WRAP PARTY.

THEN, UM...

YOU DO? THAT'S GREAT.

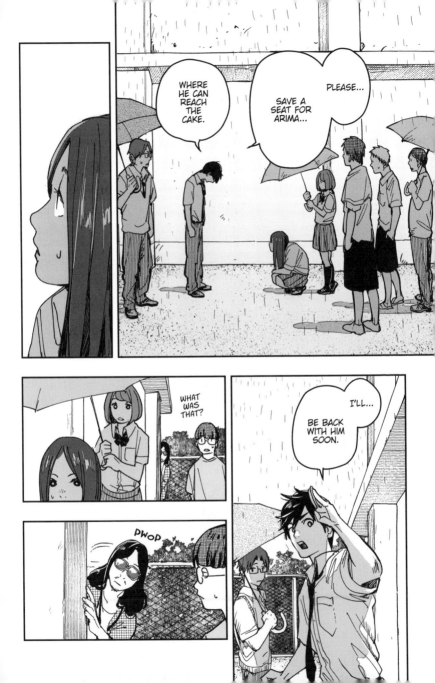

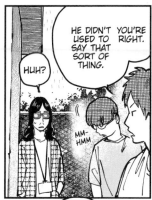

HUH?

HE DIDN'T USED TO SAY THAT SORT OF THING.

YOU'RE RIGHT.

MM-HMM

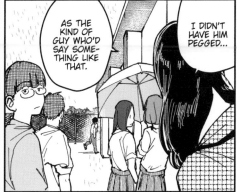

AS THE KIND OF GUY WHO'D SAY SOMETHING LIKE THAT.

I DIDN'T HAVE HIM PEGGED...

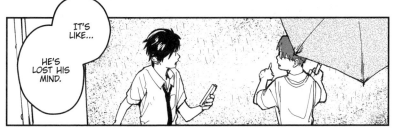

IT'S LIKE...

HE'S LOST HIS MIND.

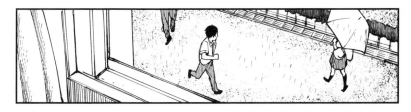

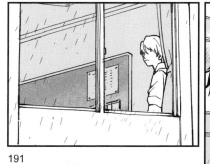

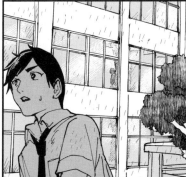

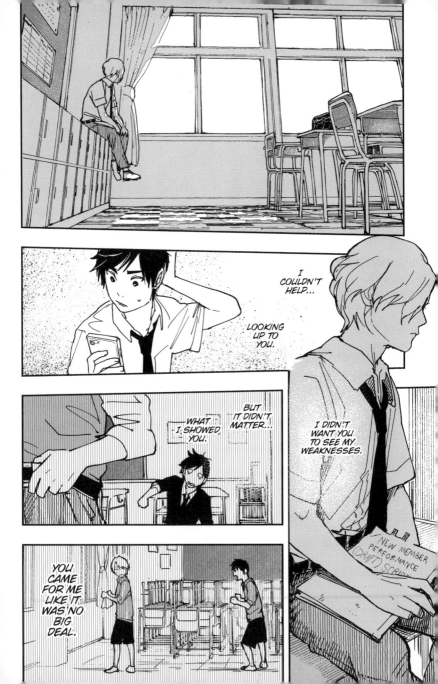

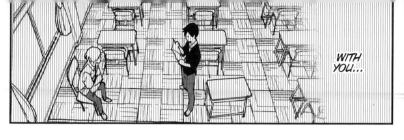

WITH YOU...

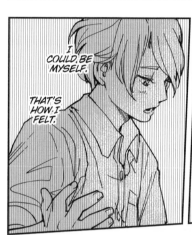

I COULD BE MYSELF.

THAT'S HOW I FELT.

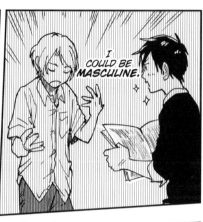

I COULD BE MASCULINE.

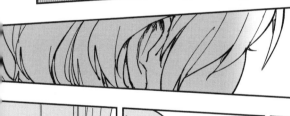

IT WAS REFRESHING.

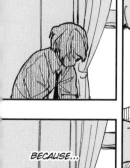

BECAUSE...

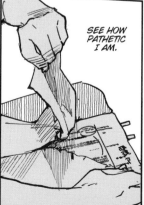

SEE HOW PATHETIC I AM.

I REALLY CAN'T LET YOU...

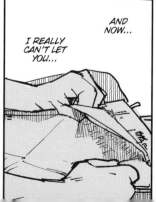

AND NOW...

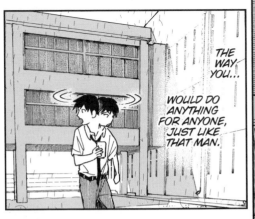

THE WAY YOU...

WOULD DO ANYTHING FOR ANYONE, JUST LIKE THAT MAN.

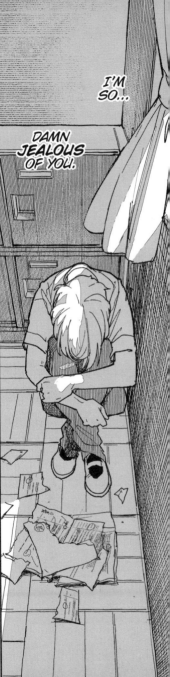

I'M SO...

DAMN **JEALOUS** OF YOU.

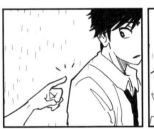

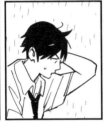

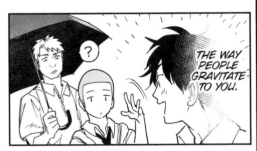

THE WAY PEOPLE GRAVITATE TO YOU.

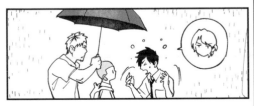

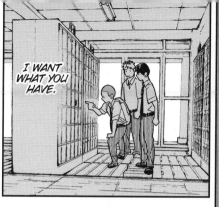

I WANT WHAT YOU HAVE.

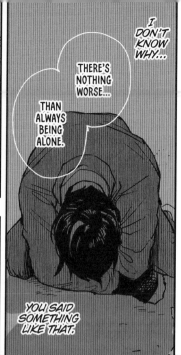

I DON'T KNOW WHY...

THERE'S NOTHING WORSE...

THAN ALWAYS BEING ALONE.

YOU SAID SOMETHING LIKE THAT.

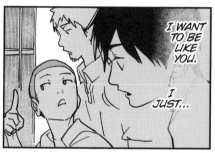

I WANT TO BE LIKE YOU.

I JUST...

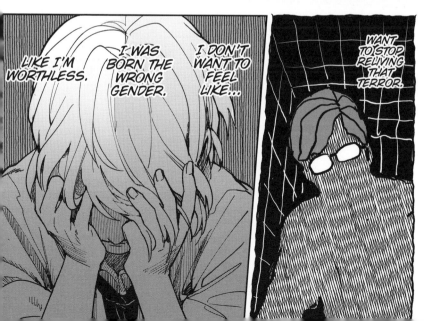

LIKE I'M WORTHLESS.

I WAS BORN THE WRONG GENDER.

I DON'T WANT TO FEEL LIKE...

WANT TO STOP RELIVING THAT TERROR.

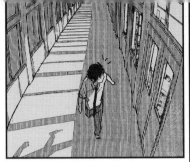

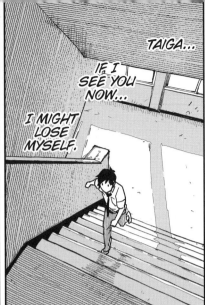

TAIGA...

IF I SEE YOU NOW...

I MIGHT LOSE MYSELF.

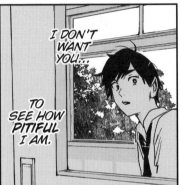

I DON'T WANT YOU...

TO SEE HOW PITIFUL I AM.

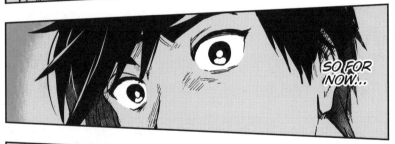

SO FOR NOW...

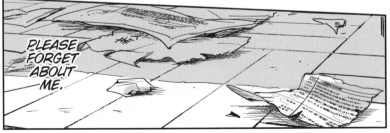

PLEASE FORGET ABOUT ME.

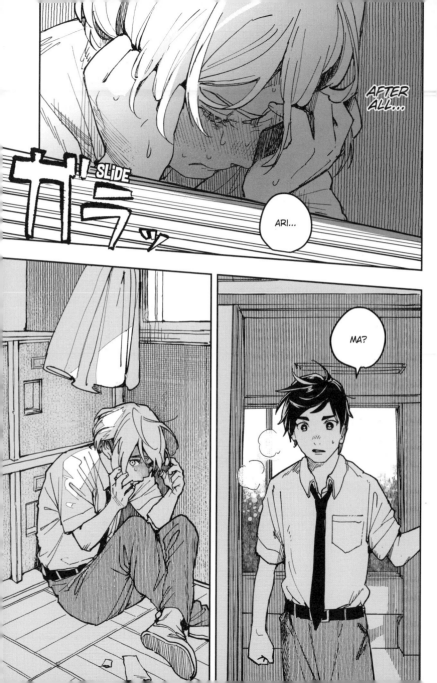

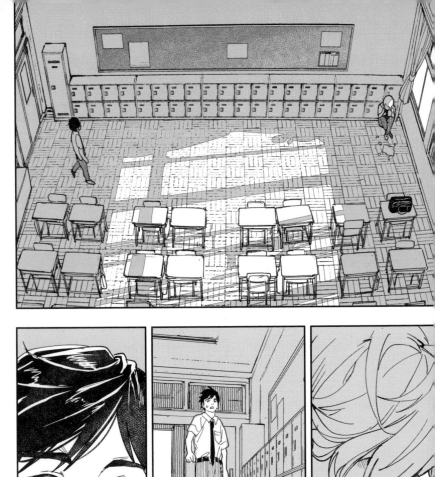

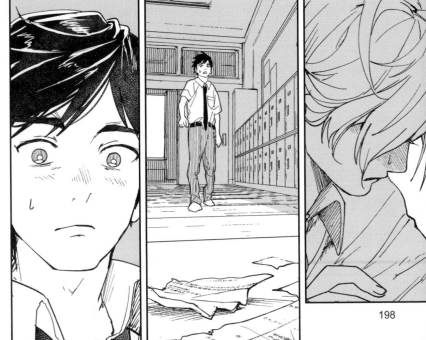

198

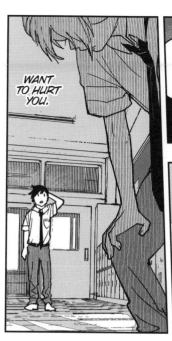

WANT TO HURT YOU.

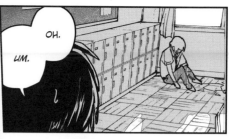

OH.

UM.

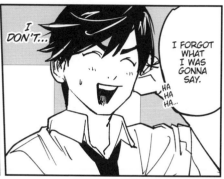

I DON'T...

I FORGOT WHAT I WAS GONNA SAY.

HA HA HA...

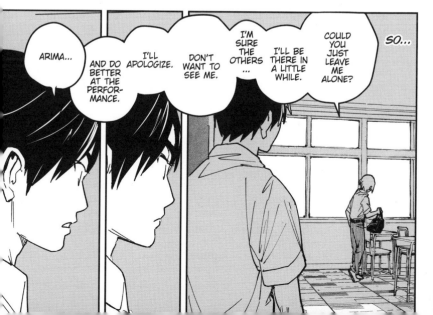

ARIMA...

AND DO BETTER AT THE PERFOR-MANCE.

I'LL APOLOGIZE.

DON'T WANT TO SEE ME.

I'M SURE THE OTHERS ...

I'LL BE THERE IN A LITTLE WHILE.

COULD YOU JUST LEAVE ME ALONE?

SO...

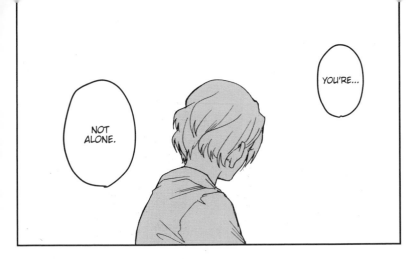

YOU'RE...

NOT ALONE.

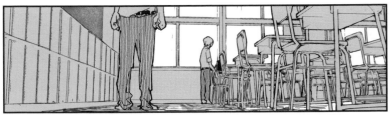

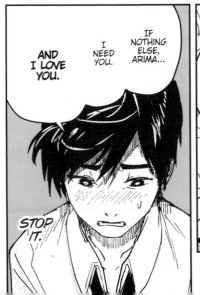

AND I LOVE YOU.

I NEED YOU.

IF NOTHING ELSE, ARIMA...

STOP IT.

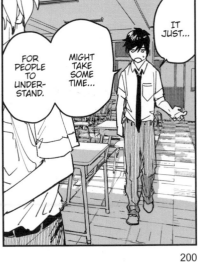

FOR PEOPLE TO UNDER-STAND.

MIGHT TAKE SOME TIME...

IT JUST...

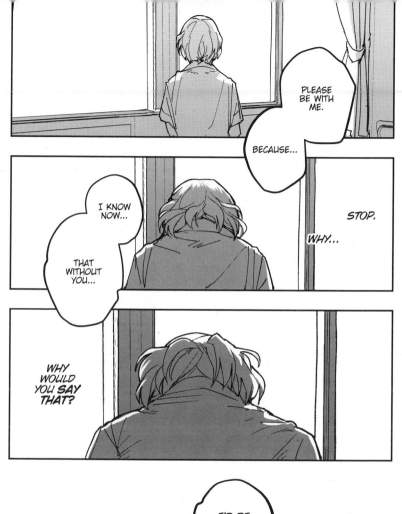
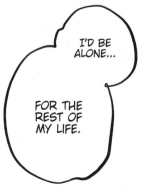

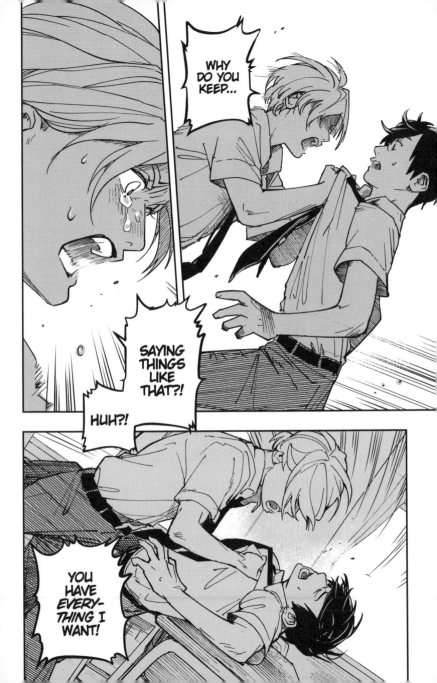

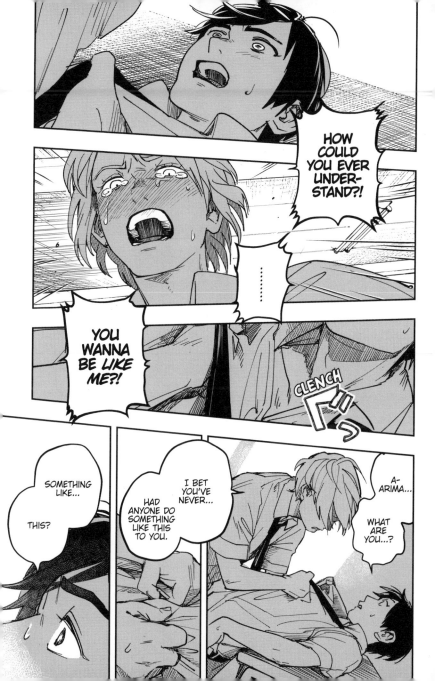

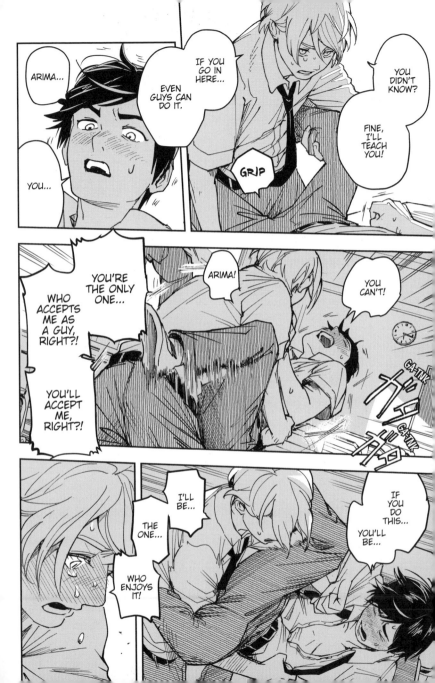

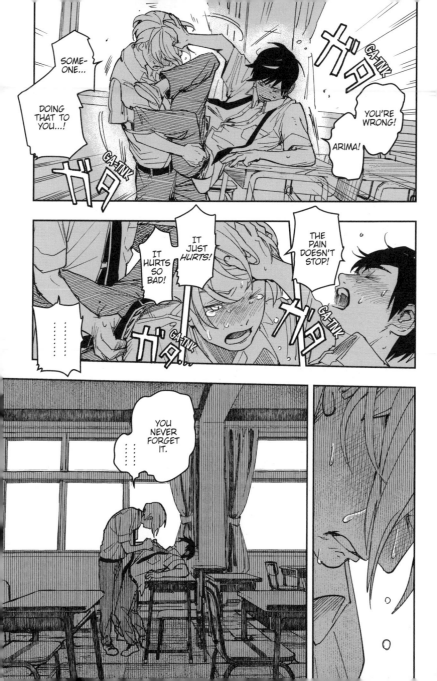

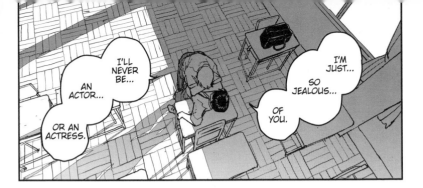

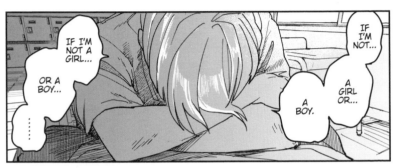

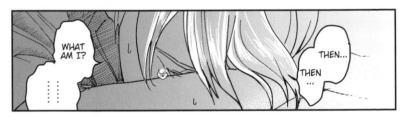

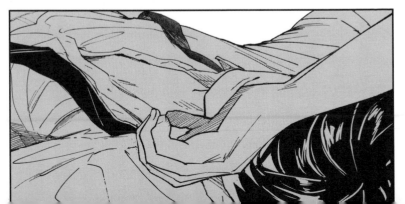

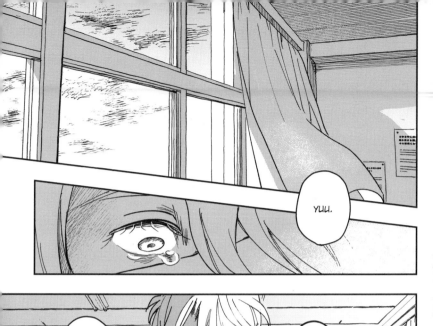

YUU.

YOUR FIRST NAME IS...

YUU, ISN'T IT?

YUU.

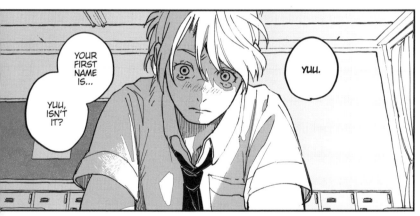

PLEASE JUST BE "YUU."

B-BECAUSE...

NOT THE "YUU" THAT MAKES UP THE WORD FOR ACTOR OR ACTRESS.

PLEASE.

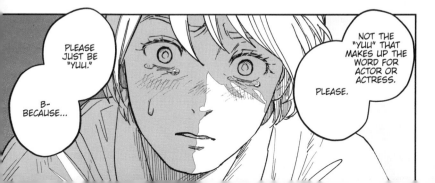

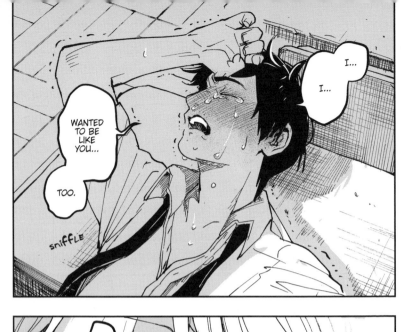

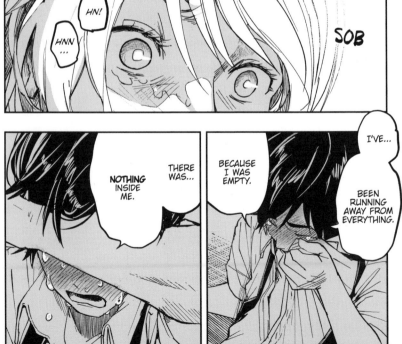

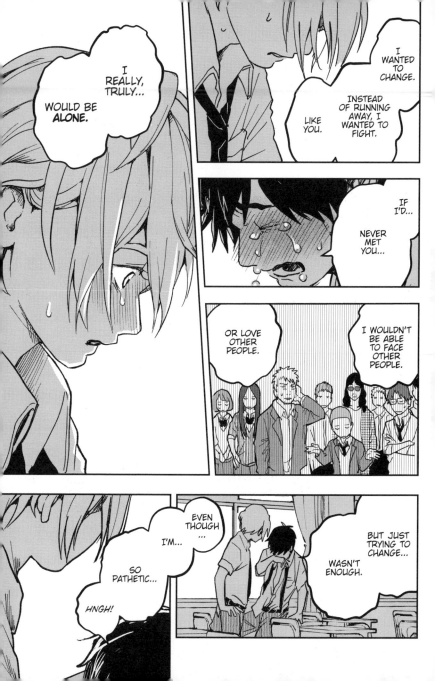

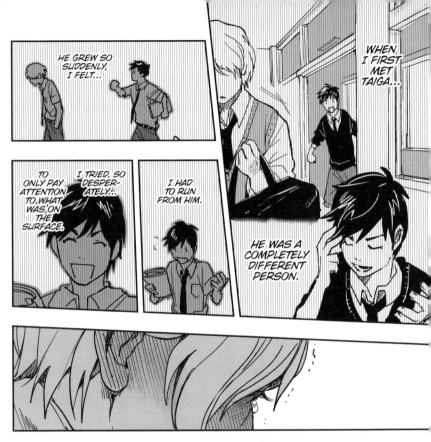

WHEN I FIRST MET TAIGA...

HE GREW SO SUDDENLY, I FELT...

TO ONLY PAY ATTENTION TO WHAT WAS ON THE SURFACE.

I TRIED, SO DESPERATELY...

I HAD TO RUN FROM HIM.

HE WAS A COMPLETELY DIFFERENT PERSON.

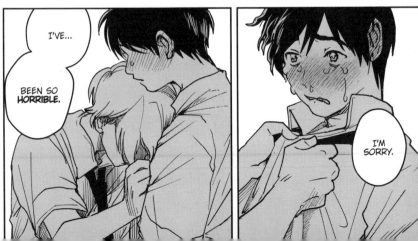

I'VE...

BEEN SO HORRIBLE.

I'M SORRY.

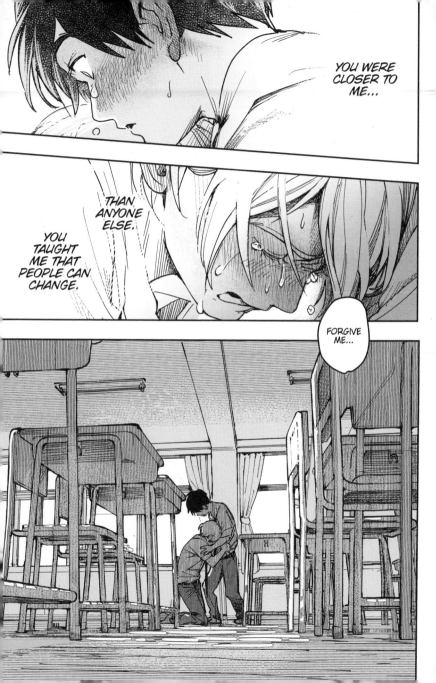

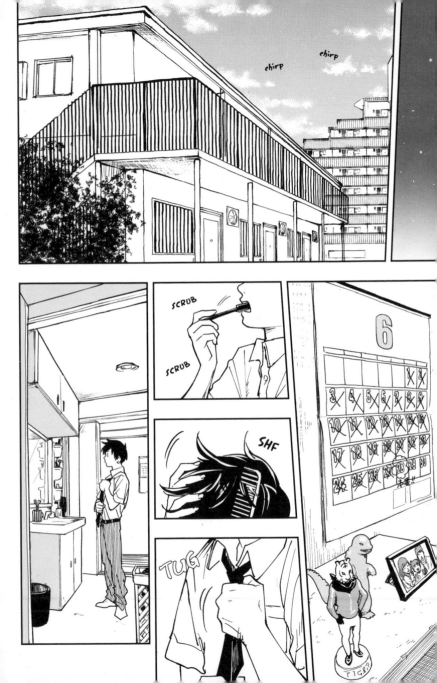

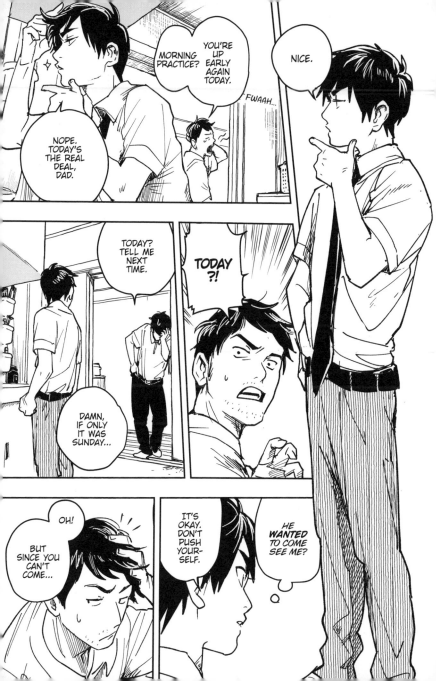

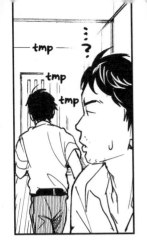

...?

tmp

tmp

tmp

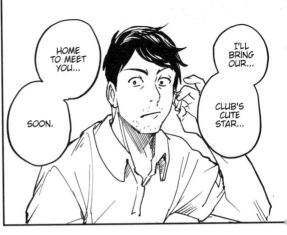

HOME TO MEET YOU...

SOON.

I'LL BRING OUR...

CLUB'S CUTE STAR...

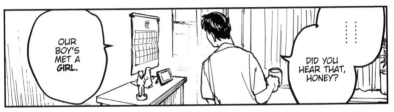

OUR BOY'S MET A GIRL.

DID YOU HEAR THAT, HONEY?

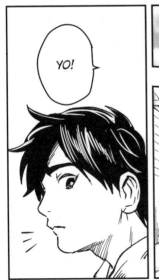

YO!

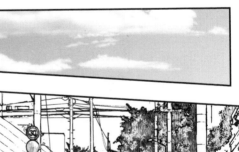

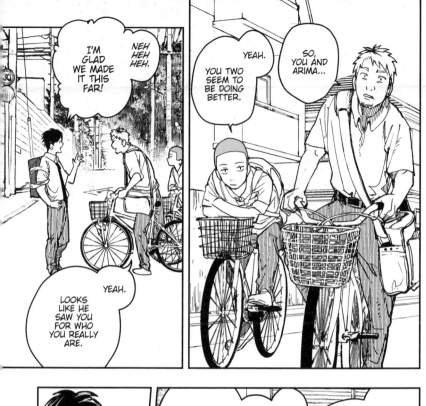

I'M GLAD WE MADE IT THIS FAR!

NEH HEH HEH.

YEAH.

YOU TWO SEEM TO BE DOING BETTER.

SO, YOU AND ARIMA...

YEAH.

LOOKS LIKE HE SAW YOU FOR WHO YOU REALLY ARE.

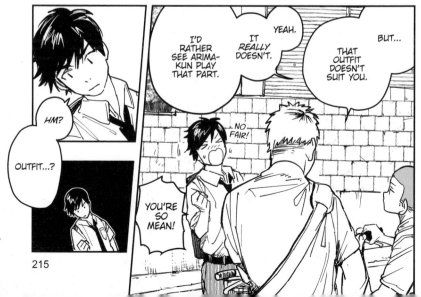

HM?

OUTFIT...?

I'D RATHER SEE ARIMA-KUN PLAY THAT PART.

IT REALLY DOESN'T.

YEAH.

BUT...

THAT OUTFIT DOESN'T SUIT YOU.

NO FAIR!

YOU'RE SO MEAN!

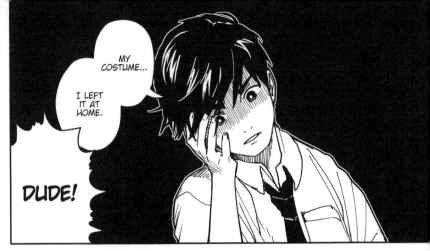

MY COSTUME...

I LEFT IT AT HOME.

DUDE!

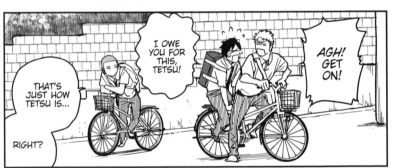

THAT'S JUST HOW TETSU IS...

RIGHT?

I OWE YOU FOR THIS, TETSU!

AGH! GET ON!

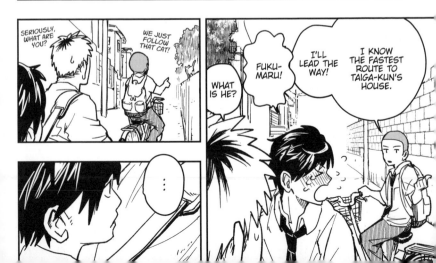

SERIOUSLY, WHAT ARE YOU?

WE JUST FOLLOW THAT CAT!

WHAT IS HE?

FUKU-MARU!

I'LL LEAD THE WAY!

I KNOW THE FASTEST ROUTE TO TAIGA-KUN'S HOUSE.

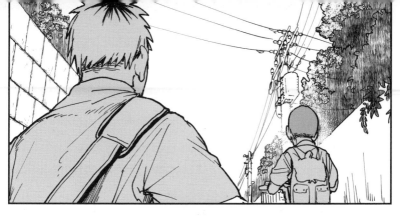

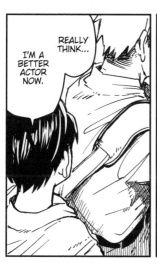

I'M A BETTER ACTOR NOW.

REALLY THINK...

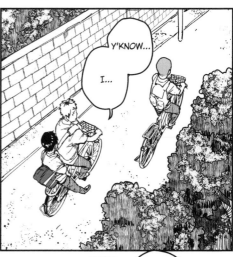

Y'KNOW...

I...

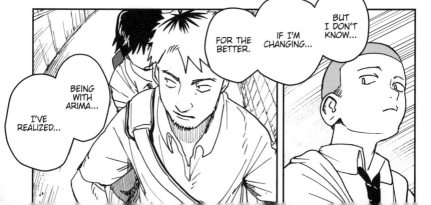

I'VE REALIZED...

BEING WITH ARIMA...

FOR THE BETTER.

IF I'M CHANGING...

BUT I DON'T KNOW...

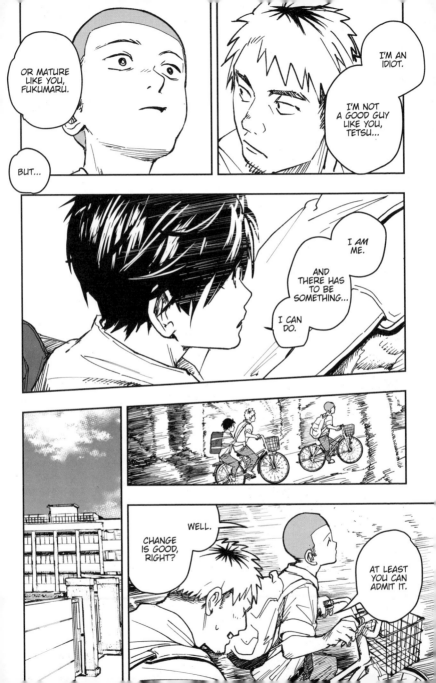

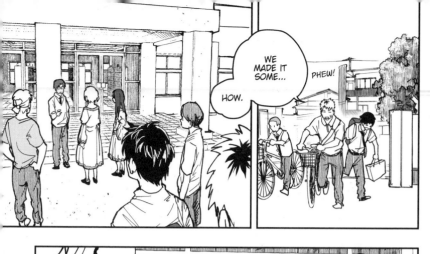

WE MADE IT SOME...

PHEW!

HOW.

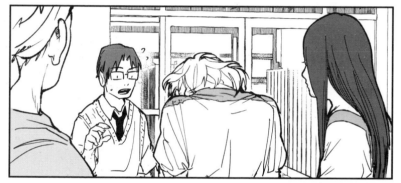

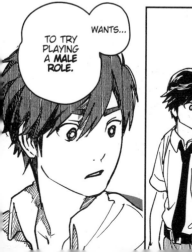

WANTS...

TO TRY PLAYING A **MALE ROLE.**

AFTER TODAY'S SHOW...

MARIA-SAMA...

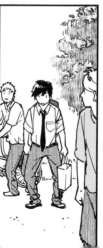

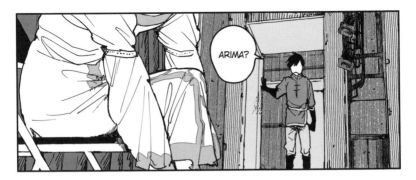

ARIMA?

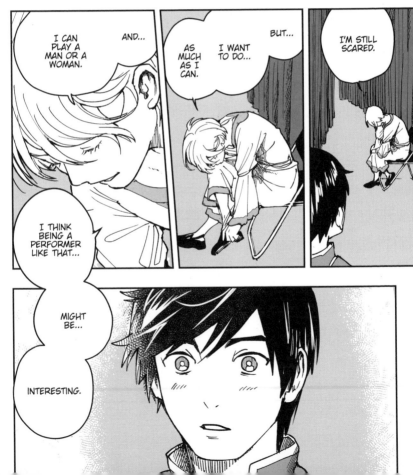

I CAN PLAY A MAN OR A WOMAN.

AND...

AS MUCH AS I CAN.

I WANT TO DO...

BUT...

I'M STILL SCARED.

I THINK BEING A PERFORMER LIKE THAT...

MIGHT BE...

INTERESTING.

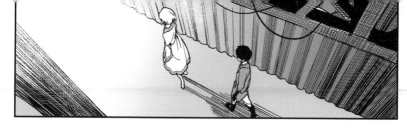
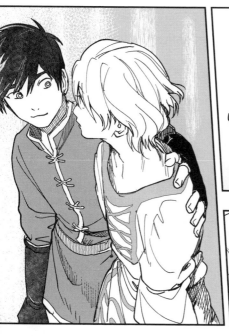
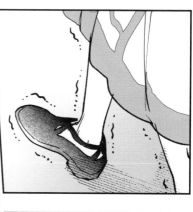
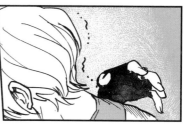
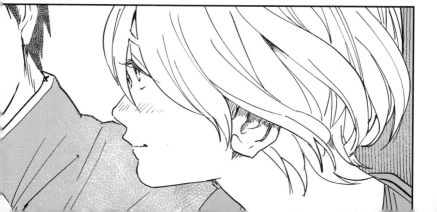

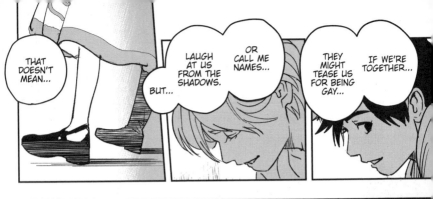

THAT DOESN'T MEAN...

BUT... LAUGH AT US FROM THE SHADOWS. OR CALL ME NAMES...

THEY MIGHT TEASE US FOR BEING GAY... IF WE'RE TOGETHER...

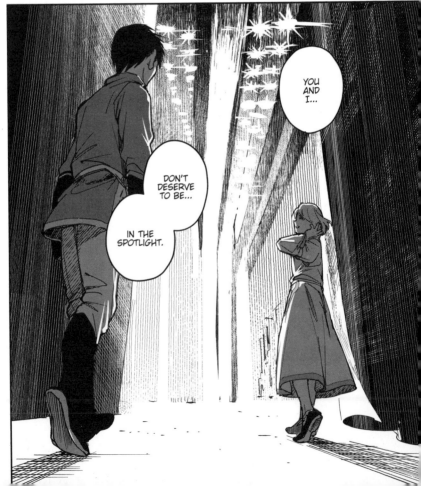

YOU AND I...

DON'T DESERVE TO BE...

IN THE SPOTLIGHT.

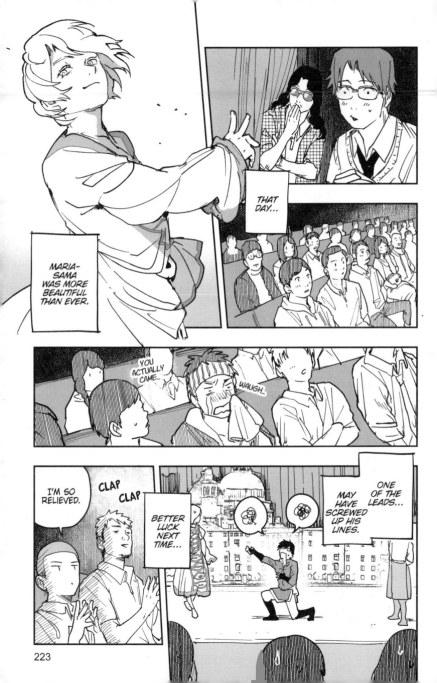

MARIA-SAMA WAS MORE BEAUTIFUL THAN EVER.

THAT DAY...

YOU ACTUALLY CAME...

WAUGH...

I'M SO RELIEVED.

CLAP CLAP

BETTER LUCK NEXT TIME...

ONE OF THE LEADS...

MAY HAVE SCREWED UP HIS LINES.

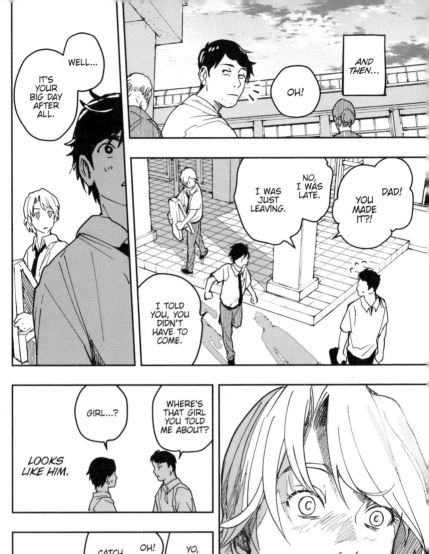

WELL...

IT'S YOUR BIG DAY AFTER ALL.

AND THEN...

OH!

DAD! YOU MADE IT?!

NO, I WAS LATE.

I WAS JUST LEAVING.

I TOLD YOU, YOU DIDN'T HAVE TO COME.

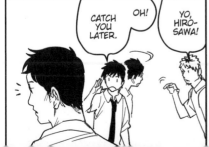

LOOKS LIKE HIM.

GIRL...?

WHERE'S THAT GIRL YOU TOLD ME ABOUT?

CATCH YOU LATER.

OH!

YO, HIRO-SAWA!

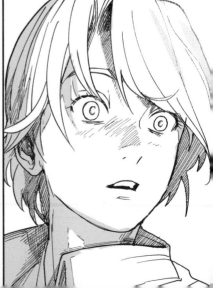

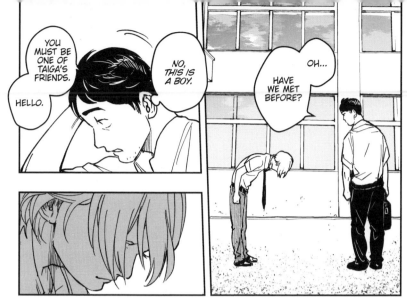

YOU MUST BE ONE OF TAIGA'S FRIENDS.

HELLO.

NO, THIS IS A BOY.

OH...

HAVE WE MET BEFORE?

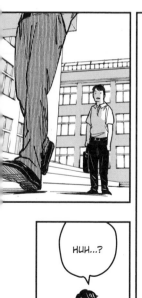

THERE'S NO REASON HE...

CAN'T HAVE A **BOYFRIEND.**

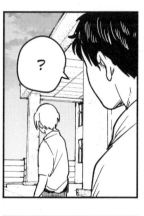

?

HUH...?

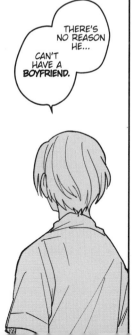

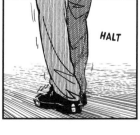

HALT

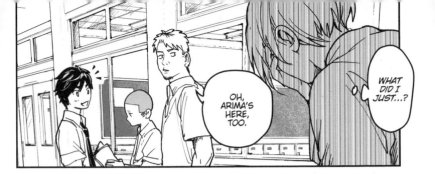

OH, ARIMA'S HERE, TOO.

WHAT DID I JUST...?

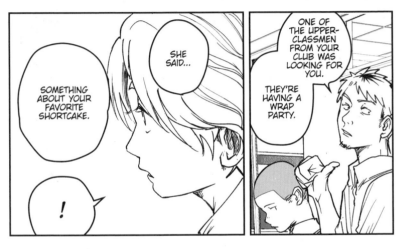

SHE SAID...

SOMETHING ABOUT YOUR FAVORITE SHORTCAKE.

!

ONE OF THE UPPER-CLASSMEN FROM YOUR CLUB WAS LOOKING FOR YOU.

THEY'RE HAVING A WRAP PARTY.

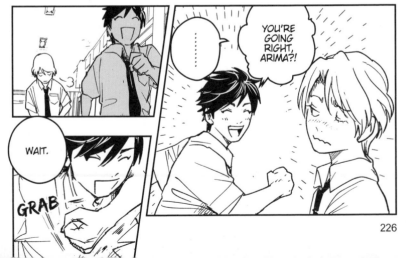

· · · · · · · ·

YOU'RE GOING RIGHT, ARIMA?!

WAIT.

GRAB

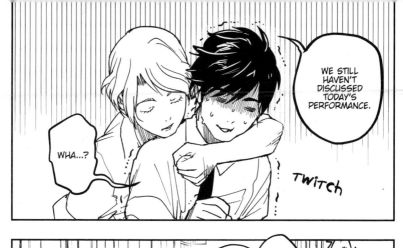

WE STILL HAVEN'T DISCUSSED TODAY'S PERFORMANCE.

WHA...?

TWITCH

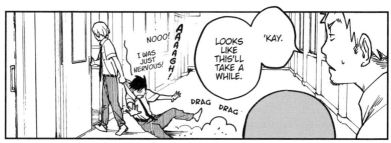

NOOO!

I WAS JUST NERVOUS!

AAAAGH!

LOOKS LIKE THIS'LL TAKE A WHILE.

'KAY.

DRAG DRAG

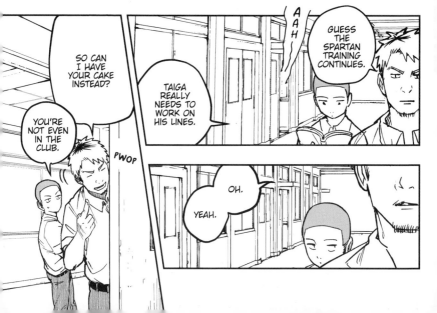

SO CAN I HAVE YOUR CAKE INSTEAD?

YOU'RE NOT EVEN IN THE CLUB.

PWOP

TAIGA REALLY NEEDS TO WORK ON HIS LINES.

A AH

GUESS THE SPARTAN TRAINING CONTINUES.

OH.

YEAH.

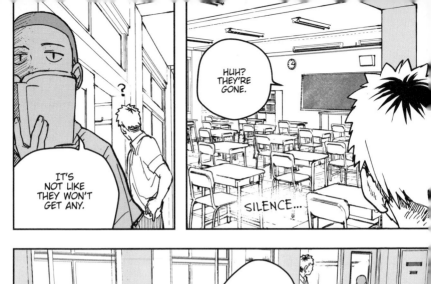

HUH? THEY'RE GONE.

IT'S NOT LIKE THEY WON'T GET ANY.

SILENCE...

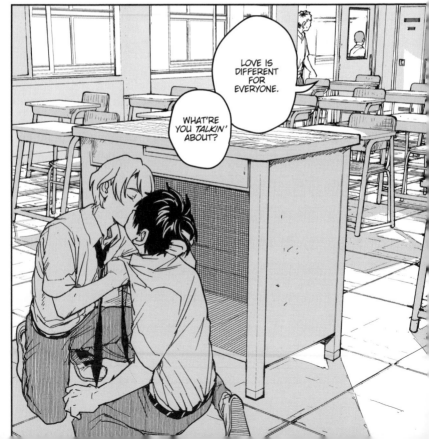

LOVE IS DIFFERENT FOR EVERYONE.

WHAT'RE YOU *TALKIN'* ABOUT?

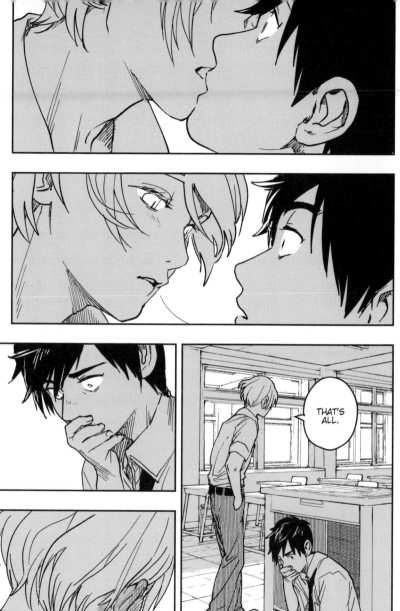

THAT'S
ALL.

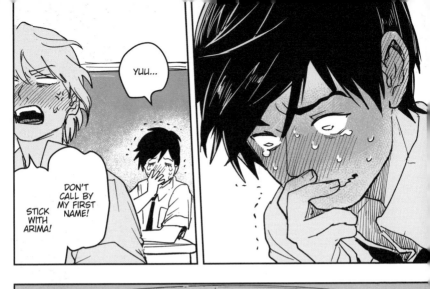

YUU...

DON'T CALL BY MY FIRST NAME!

STICK WITH ARIMA!

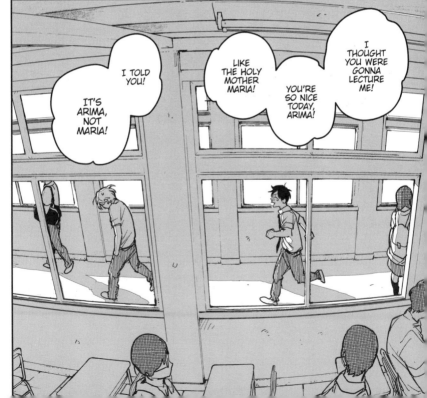

I TOLD YOU!

IT'S ARIMA, NOT MARIA!

LIKE THE HOLY MOTHER MARIA!

YOU'RE SO NICE TODAY, ARIMA!

I THOUGHT YOU WERE GONNA LECTURE ME!

Boy Meets Maria

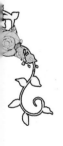

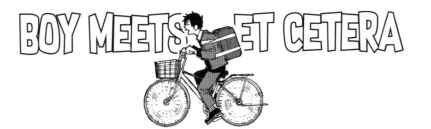

BOY MEETS ET CETERA

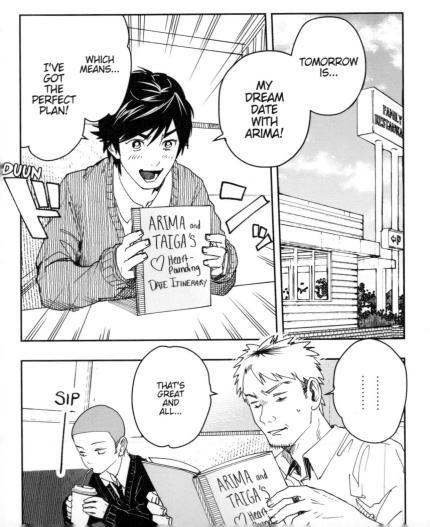

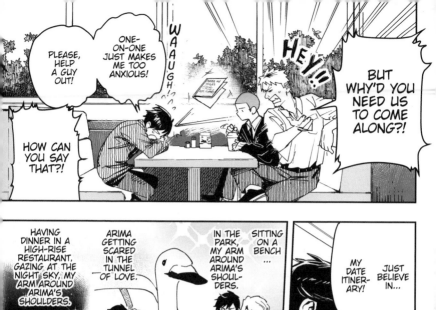

PLEASE, HELP A GUY OUT!

ONE-ON-ONE JUST MAKES ME TOO ANXIOUS!

WAAUGH

HEY!!

BUT WHY'D YOU NEED US TO COME ALONG?!

HOW CAN YOU SAY THAT?!

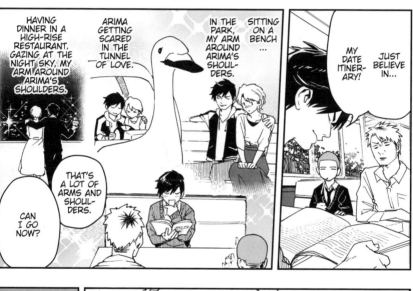

HAVING DINNER IN A HIGH-RISE RESTAURANT, GAZING AT THE NIGHT SKY, MY ARM AROUND ARIMA'S SHOULDERS.

ARIMA GETTING SCARED IN THE TUNNEL OF LOVE.

IN THE PARK, MY ARM AROUND ARIMA'S SHOULDERS.

SITTING ON A BENCH...

MY DATE ITINERARY!

JUST BELIEVE IN...

THAT'S A LOT OF ARMS AND SHOULDERS.

CAN I GO NOW?

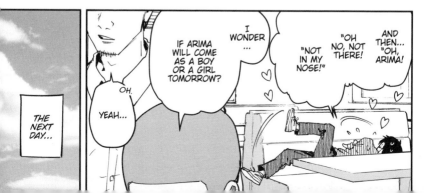

IF ARIMA WILL COME AS A BOY OR A GIRL TOMORROW?

I WONDER...

"NOT IN MY NOSE!"

"OH NO, NOT THERE!

AND THEN... "OH, ARIMA!

OH. YEAH...

THE NEXT DAY...

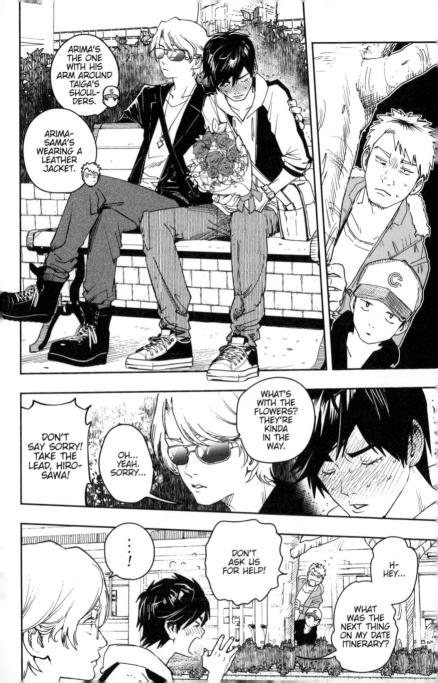

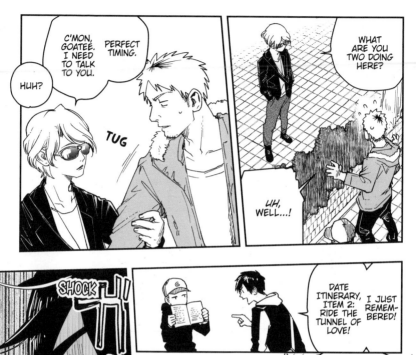

C'MON, GOATEE. I NEED TO TALK TO YOU.

PERFECT TIMING.

HUH?

TUG

WHAT ARE YOU TWO DOING HERE?

UH, WELL...!

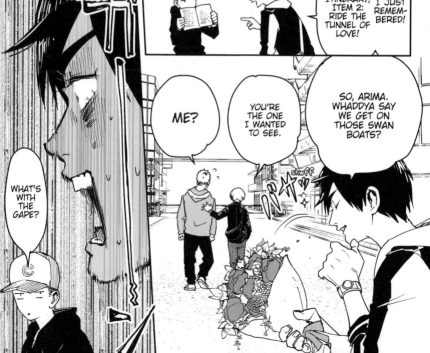

SHOCK

DATE ITINERARY, ITEM 2: RIDE THE TUNNEL OF LOVE!

I JUST REMEMBERED!

ME?

YOU'RE THE ONE I WANTED TO SEE.

SO, ARIMA. WHADDYA SAY WE GET ON THOSE SWAN BOATS?

shwff

WHAT'S WITH THE GAPE?

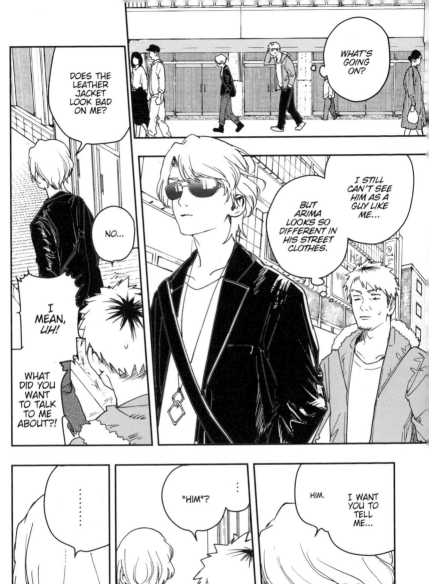

DOES THE LEATHER JACKET LOOK BAD ON ME?

WHAT'S GOING ON?

NO...

I STILL CAN'T SEE HIM AS A GUY LIKE ME...

BUT ARIMA LOOKS SO DIFFERENT IN HIS STREET CLOTHES.

I MEAN, UH!

WHAT DID YOU WANT TO TALK TO ME ABOUT?!

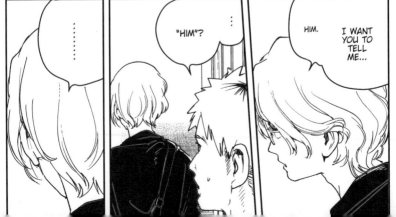

· · · · · · · ·

"HIM"?

HIM.

I WANT YOU TO TELL ME...

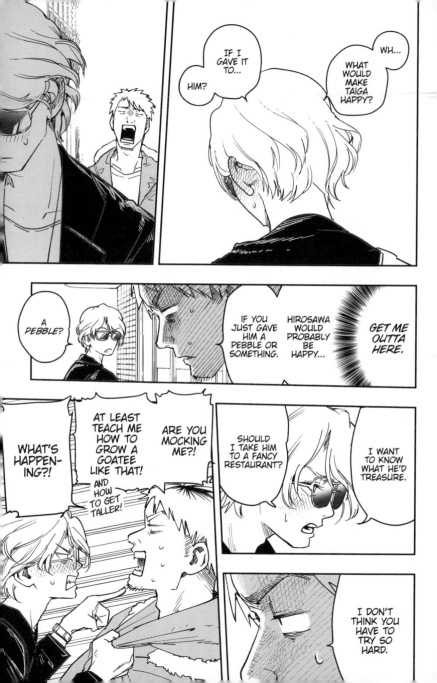

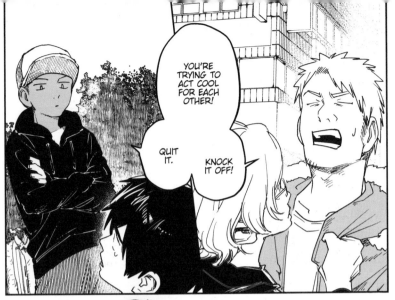

YOU'RE TRYING TO ACT COOL FOR EACH OTHER!

QUIT IT.

KNOCK IT OFF!

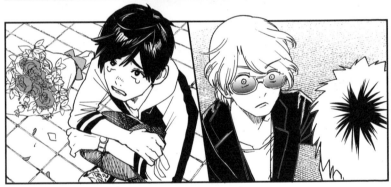

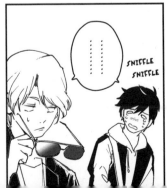

· · · · ·

SNIFFLE SNIFFLE

AND ARIMA, I DON'T WANNA SEE YOU WITH A GOATEE.

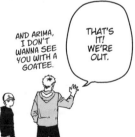

THAT'S IT! WE'RE OUT.

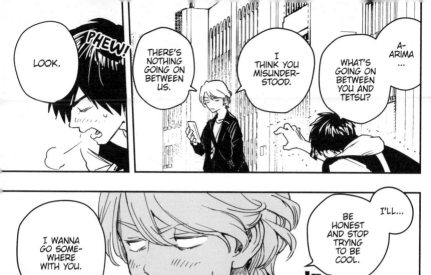

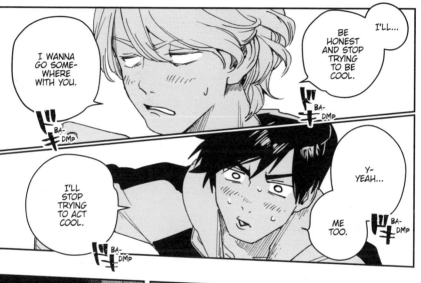

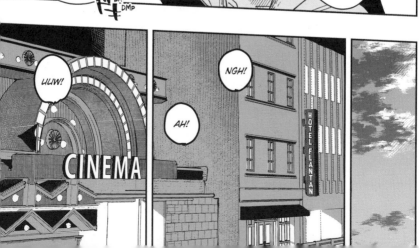

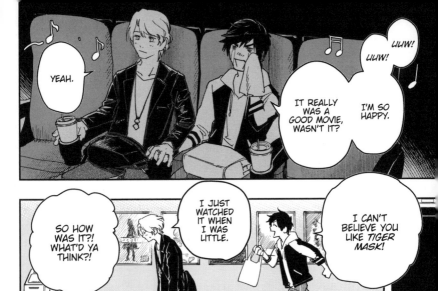

YEAH.

IT REALLY WAS A GOOD MOVIE, WASN'T IT?

I'M SO HAPPY.

UUW! UUW!

SO HOW WAS IT?! WHAT'D YA THINK?!

I JUST WATCHED IT WHEN I WAS LITTLE.

I CAN'T BELIEVE YOU LIKE *TIGER MASK!*

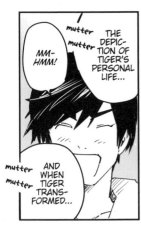

MM-HMM!

mutter mutter THE DEPICTION OF TIGER'S PERSONAL LIFE...

mutter mutter AND WHEN TIGER TRANSFORMED...

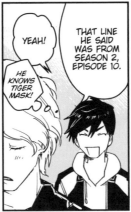

YEAH!

HE KNOWS TIGER MASK!

THAT LINE HE SAID WAS FROM SEASON 2, EPISODE 10.

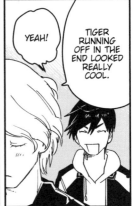

YEAH!

TIGER RUNNING OFF IN THE END LOOKED REALLY COOL.

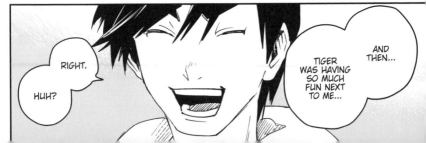

RIGHT.

HUH?

TIGER WAS HAVING SO MUCH FUN NEXT TO ME...

AND THEN...

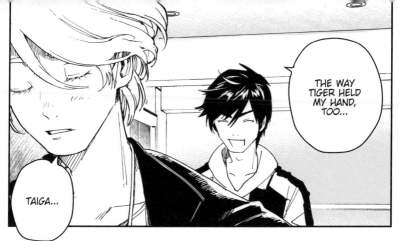

THE WAY TIGER HELD MY HAND, TOO...

TAIGA...

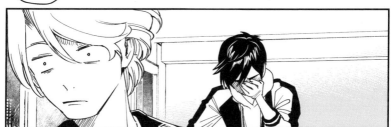

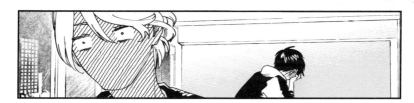

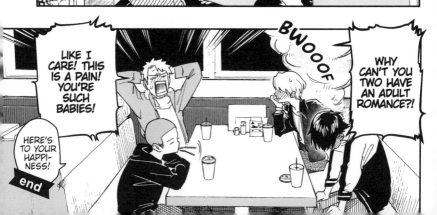

LIKE I CARE! THIS IS A PAIN! YOU'RE SUCH BABIES!

HERE'S TO YOUR HAPPINESS!

BWOOOF

WHY CAN'T YOU TWO HAVE AN ADULT ROMANCE?!

end

SEVEN SEAS ENTERTAINMENT PRESENTS

Boy Meets Maria

story and art by PEYO

TRANSLATION
Amber Tamosaitis

ADAPTATION
Lora Gray

LETTERING
Danya Shevchenko

COVER DESIGN
Hanase Qi

PROOFREADER
Kurestin Armada

COPY EDITOR
Dawn Davis

EDITOR
Jenn Grunigen

PREPRESS TECHNICIAN
Rhiannon Rasmussen-Silverstein

PRODUCTION ASSOCIATE
Christa Miesner

PRODUCTION MANAGER
Lissa Pattillo

MANAGING EDITOR
Julie Davis

ASSOCIATE PUBLISHER
Adam Arnold

PUBLISHER
Jason DeAngelis

Boy Meets Maria
© PEYO 2018
Originally published in Japan in 2018 by FRANCE SHOIN Inc., Tokyo.
English Translation rights arranged with FRANCE SHOIN Inc., Tokyo,
through TOHAN CORPORATION, Tokyo

Seven Seas press and purchase enquiries can be sent to Marketing Manager Lianne
Sentar at press@gomanga.com. Information regarding the distribution and purchase of
digital editions is available from Digital Manager CK Russell at digital@gomanga.com.

Seven Seas and the Seven Seas logo are trademarks of
Seven Seas Entertainment. All rights reserved.

ISBN: 978-1-64827-645-3
Printed in Hong Kong, China
First Printing: October 2021
10 9 8 7 6 5

////// READING DIRECTIONS //////

This book reads from *right to left,*
Japanese style. If this is your first time
reading manga, you start reading from
the top right panel on each page and
take it from there. If you get lost, just
follow the numbered diagram here.
It may seem backwards at first,
but you'll get the hang of it! Have fun!!

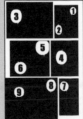

Follow us online: www.SevenSeasEntertainment.com